IT'S NOT PERSONAL!

A Guide to Anger Management

Alice J. Katz, M.S.

IT'S NOT PERSONAL!

ISBN 0-9651729-0-2

Manufactured in the United States of America
First Printing 1996

Published 1996
AJK PUBLISHING
Westport, CT

Produced by
PPC BOOKS
Westport, CT

Acknowledgments

Many people helped make this book possible. Special thanks:

- To the men and women who have shared their stories and their feelings with me in counseling sessions and in group workshops. It is from them that I have gathered the ideas that make up this book.
- To my husband Phil for helping me understand his anger, my own, and that of any two people attempting to interact with each other.
- To my children Melissa and Adam; and to Janice Weinberg, Regina Krummel, Barbara Levine, and the rest of my family and friends for their input and for encouraging me to keep the manuscript alive and not give it up.
- To my sister Dorri Jacobs and to Diana Potter for their fine job of editing and their invaluable support.

The people portrayed throughout the book are
composites, as are their stories, so that the privacy
of the real individuals may be protected.

Table of Contents

Introduction   i

Part One: **FEELING ANGRY**
  1 Understanding Your Anger   1
  2 Identifying Your Anger   11
  3 Feeling Less Angry at Others   21
  4 Feeling Less Angry at Home   31

Part Two: **EXPRESSING ANGRY FEELINGS**
  5 Expressing Anger Without Fear   42
  6 Becoming More Direct   59
  7 Ending Your Aggression   73

Part Three: **COPING WITH ANGRY PEOPLE**
  8 Seeing Hidden Anger in Others   82
  9 Coping with Manipulators   90
 10 Coping with Aggressive People   101

Part Four: **MAKING POSITIVE CHANGES**
 11 Being Less Angry at Yourself   114
 12 Asserting Yourself   124
 13 Taking Charge   143
 14 Reducing Stress   152
 15 Assessing Your Progress   165

Introduction

Wouldn't you love to stay calm when you encounter criticism, hostility, rejection, or abuse from people, or when you find that they don't meet your expectations? Wouldn't it be good to see and hear what they are doing and not take it personally?

The key to mental and physical health is being able to do just that no matter how other people treat you. Then, your ego stays intact, you feel great, you have boundless energy, and you are filled with joy. You love living and every new experience is a treasure. Your anger, fears, anxieties, discontent, and self-destructive tendencies are minimal.

What a world this would be if everyone took things less personally! No more greed, revenge, hatred, or violence, and maybe even no more wars!

As it stands now, the number of angry people of all ages and backgrounds who express their anger violently seems to be increasing everywhere, as evidenced by the frequency of street muggings, rapes in the park, residential robberies, drive-by shootings, subway bombings, arsons, domestic batterings, murders, knifings, and civil wars.

Angry people make the world a scary place. They hurt strangers and friends with insulting words, rude behavior, lack of consideration, selfishness, and sometimes violent behavior. Their anger sends out negative energy that upsets those around them. Angry people hurt themselves too, because their anger festers inside like a wound, engulfing them and growing larger with time. Their anger weakens their immune systems, and they get ulcers, colds, flu, allergies, exhaustion, and possibly depression.

A world made up of people who keep their anger at a minimum and express it without attacking each other will be one that is safe and sane. To do that, everyone must first become less competitive, less revengeful, and, above all, less apt to take everything personally.

That may be hard to do. It takes a lot of work to go through a day in a complex society without having your anger triggered. There are daily encounters with frustrating situations, such as traffic jams, bad weather, sudden illness, job loss, and cars and appliances that break down. There are daily encounters with irritating people who make clerical errors, overcharge for their services, hog the road, monopolize the conversation, speak rudely, make noise, hustle you, solicit you, smoke, ask personal questions, use insulting words, refuse to cooperate, let you down, criticize you, or keep you waiting on a line, on the phone, or in an office.

In spite of having all of those anger triggers in your life, it is very possible for you to learn constructive anger behavior. All you need is the desire and the willingness to work hard. That is what so many of those who attended my workshops on anger management discovered. Seeing their successes inspired me to write this book, and to make available to you and other readers the ideas and exercises used in the program.

Whatever it is that you want to change about your anger, you can. Maybe you are angry too often; maybe you express your anger too explosively; maybe you never know when you are angry; maybe you are afraid to express your anger. If you want to, you can get to a point where you:

- Feel your anger and know when you feel it, rather than being unaware of what you feel.

- Have only moderate amounts of anger, rather than extremes of rage.

- Are angry only some of the time, rather than most of the time.

- Express your anger when you choose to express it, rather than censoring it.

- Express your anger in a non-hurtful way, rather than attacking others with it.

- Take nothing that people say or do personally, rather than feeling hurt.

IT'S NOT PERSONAL! contains anecdotes, charts, questionnaires, and imagery exercises to help you achieve these goals. The people described in the anecdotes are actually composites of the many hundreds who sought counseling and attended workshops to change their anger behavior because it was hurting their relationships and their health. How they handled their various situations can provide you with guidelines for dealing with other people.

There are four parts to the book:

Part One discusses what anger is, what it feels like, why you get angry, and what new ideas can lead to feeling less angry at other people and at yourself.

Part Two is about expressing your anger without fear, and helps you see if you are expressing it in a way that is passive-aggressive or aggressive.

Part Three discusses the ways you can deal with angry people who may hide their anger or express it by being manipulative or abusive.

Part Four shows you how making life changes, such as improving your self-image, becoming assertive, saying no without guilt, making choices, becoming more independent, increasing pleasure, slowing down, and letting go can make you less angry.

The basis of this book is to help you look at the thoughts and beliefs that trigger your angry feelings and lead to your anger behavior. You get angry when you believe that people are attacking your ego, your property, your freedom, or your body. The problem is that what you believe you will perceive, and, unless you base your perceptions on reality, they may be distorted by what you think.

You may not be able to avoid people who seem abusive, but you can change the way you think about them. You can learn to make less negative assumptions about what motivates their behavior. You can learn to have more realistic expectations about them.

As you read, keep in mind what you want to change about your anger. When you answer the questions in the progress test at the end, see how many of these changes have been accomplished.

The questionnaires in each chapter of the book are meant to increase your awareness about how you handle your anger. It is probably more beneficial to fill them in as you come upon them, but you could read the whole book first. Before you put in your answers, be sure to read the instructions and the information preceding each item. Write on the page in the space provided, so you can refer to your answers in the future. Give the appropriate response. Try not to make judgments about your feelings or your behavior. Remember there are no right answers, only your answers.

When you do the exercises, go slowly, because there is a lot to think about. If it takes you weeks rather than days to finish reading, you will have more time between each section to process your new insights.

When you do finish, practice what you have learned about your anger, and be aware of any changes you are making. You might want to retake the questionnaires and put your answers on a piece of paper. Then you can compare them to your earlier ones and see if you have made any progress. You are likely to find that changes in your thinking about anger has led to changes in your behavior and in your reaction to situations.

Be patient with yourself, though. Constructive change begins with insight and awareness, and actual change in behavior happens slowly. If you are reading this book, you probably are motivated to make changes.

It is sincerely hoped that this book will help you and many others to be less angry. While no book can take the place of a counseling program, it can start you on a journey toward effective anger behavior. When you take charge of your anger no matter what happens in your life, you make it work for you instead of against you. If, in time you become less angry and take things less personally, you send out better messages to those you meet, which helps create a gentler world. If so, **IT'S NOT PERSONAL!** will have served its purpose.

Part One

FEELING ANGRY

You are about to embark on a journey that will help you take charge of your anger. This section will show you what anger is, how your angry feelings develop, and what can trigger your anger. It shows you how to change the beliefs, perceptions and thoughts on which your angry feelings are based so you can take things less personally and feel less angry with others.

1. UNDERSTANDING YOUR ANGER

Bad Anger

It is not that pleasant to feel angry with someone or be angry about some situation. Does that mean anger is a negative emotion and you should strive to be anger-free?

Not necessarily. Feeling angry can be harmful, but it can also be good. It really depends on the frequency, the intensity, and the duration of your anger; what you are angry about; and how appropriate it is to feel angry in a particular situation.

In the following circumstances, feeling angry can be harmful to yourself and to others:

■ **When there is no danger, anger is bad...**

In nature, creatures defend against physical threats to their body, territory, offspring, or freedom. Some run away or blend in with the environment so as not to be seen. Some fight back by emitting a poison, an offensive odor or a warning sound. Some sting, scratch or bite their enemy. It is questionable whether they feel angry or their reaction to danger is instinctive.

As a human, you also react instinctively to being physically threatened, but unlike animals, you can feel threatened by words and get angry about having your feelings hurt. Unlike animals, you can perceive danger when there is none, and feel hurt by someone's behavior when no hurt was intended. When you do that, your anger serves no purpose and is not appropriate.

When you blame people for attacking you when they are not, your anger is harmful. It is better to save your anger for when you really need it.

- **Anger about hate or revenge is bad...**

Animals attack each other for survival: to eat or to prevent themselves from being eaten. As a human, you may attack another human for sport, for revenge, or out of hatred. That makes your anger a dangerous emotion. Hate can cause you to attack those who have not hurt you. It is the cause of many civil and global wars. Getting revenge makes you want to inflict hurt on an attacker greater than he inflicted on you, or get even with a person who hurt you long after he has gone away. If your anger is about hate or revenge, it is harmful to you and to others.

- **Frequent anger is bad...**

Every time you feel angry, it has an effect on your body. It drains some of your energy, churns your stomach, and makes your heart race. Even if the anger you feel is not that strong, being angry very often can lead to ulcers, headaches, anxiety, depression, high blood pressure, and, as some people in the medical community believe, to heart attacks. It can also take up all of your time and make it difficult to concentrate on more important things.

- **Intense anger is bad...**

Anger that is rage can charge you up and put a strain on your heart and your digestion. Rage can also hurt your relationships, since it can lead to your screaming, yelling, and saying hurtful things to others that you may later regret. It can put you out of control so that you are no longer able to see things rationally, and give you violent thoughts that you later decide to act out.

- **Unexpressed anger is bad...**

Keeping angry feelings inside for a long time can lead to becoming depressed and unable to sleep or concentrate. You may feel listless because the energy created by the anger has nowhere to go. You may find that walking around angry puts a wall around you so that people who meet you feel shut out, rejected, and angry.

Good Anger

Feeling or expressing anger is not always bad. Under the following conditions, it is actually very good.

■ **Anger about wanting constructive change is good...**

Anger is a protest against the status quo. When your anger is about being abused by a mate, a controlling parent, an inconsiderate friend, or a critical boss, it is good because it is a demand to be treated better. If you become insistent, you can get what you want. If you do not feel angry when those things occur, you let things be as they are and you continue to be victimized.

When your anger is about seeing others mistreated, it is good because it can make you want to do things to improve the situation, such as write letters about it to political leaders and the media, join activist groups, run for local political office, or donate money to organizations fighting to correct injustice. Without anger, you are likely to do nothing and to let unfair practices continue.

■ **Anger about caring is good...**

Think about anger as wanting things to be the best for yourself or for other people in your life. You feel angry about being mistreated because you care enough about yourself to think you deserve better treatment. You feel angry about someone close to you hurting himself with drugs or alcohol, an abusive relationship, or poor performance at school or a job because you want more for him.

If someone in a close relationship with you is often angry with you, it may not be because he hates you. It may instead be for the opposite reason...that he cares a great deal about you and cannot stand to see you be hurt in any way. Getting angry may just be his way of dealing with anxiety.

■ **Anger that gives you creative energy is good...**

When you feel angry, you are charged up with extra energy that you need to release. Having an angry outburst may help discharge some of that anger. If you don't express your anger at all, it stays with you and may get in the way of your functioning .

The energy that comes from feeling angry can sometimes be channeled into other activities. If you are angry, you may play sports better than if you are not angry because you are more motivated to win. If you play tennis, you can harness your anger to slam the ball harder and to run faster on the court. In business, your anger can make you more competitive so you work harder to succeed.

The same creative energy from anger can be used during illness as a healing power. Research shows that a person who loses the will to fight a serious illness often succumbs to it sooner than a person whose anger at being sick makes him determined to get well.

Without some anger, you may be too passive and too complaisant to play to win, to meet any challenges in your life, to be expressive, or to go after what you want.

■ **Anger that makes for contact with others is good...**

Angry exchanges with someone may not be pleasant, but they are better than silence and indifference. When you tell people that you are angry with them, you make contact with them. Then, they know how you feel and what you want.

When someone tells you he is angry with you, it is better than if he feels angry and says nothing. At least you know where you stand with him and at least he is communicating.

You can see that anger is bad when it is too frequent, too strong, is about revenge and being violent, is based on distortions, or is not expressed. It is good when it is of moderate intensity, and is about justice, assertiveness, creativity, constructive change, and caring. You can work to make sure your anger is not harmful to you or to anyone else.

The Process of Becoming Angry

Anger is one of your emotions, along with happiness, sadness, and fear. All other emotions are variations of these. You feel **happy** when good things happen to you or to someone you care about, and you can express it by smiling, singing, and jumping up and down. You feel **sad** when you lose something, such as a job, a pet, or a person you care about, or when something you planned turns out differently, and you can express it by crying or moaning and letting your body sag. You feel **afraid** when you think something harmful may happen to you or to someone you care about, and you can express it by screaming, running, or cowering in a corner.

You feel **angry** when you protest against physical or emotional mistreatment, and you can express it by yelling or using words, your fists, or a weapon to hurt someone. You may feel angry more often than you feel happy, sad, or afraid, but your anger actually grows out of feeling afraid and maybe sad. What happens is:

• You become aware of someone's behavior.

• You feel afraid that it a threat to your safety and you will lose something you value.

• You feel wronged and blame this person for intending to hurt you.

• You feel sad and disappointed that he has not lived up to your expectations.

When you go beyond fear and disappointment about a perceived threat by someone, either:

• You object to being mistreated by him and you feel angry with him. (You may express your anger or keep quiet)

• or You think it is your fault, and you get angry with yourself instead of him.

On a diagram, this process looks like this:

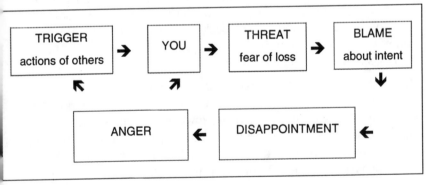

To explain further what happens:

Stage One: **Trigger** (what someone does that results in your anger)

The trigger for your anger is what you see or hear someone do. As long as you are personally affected by it, even if the words are for someone else, you can feel angry. In fact, you can get angry about what someone on television or in a movie says or what is said about someone in a newspaper article. Most of the time, your anger will be triggered by the behavior of a person you know.

Consider the case of a woman named Nancy. She was sitting at home in the evening with her husband Joe. They were in the den, and she was telling him about an experience at work. Before she could finish, he turned on the television and began to watch it. Nancy immediately felt rejected and ignored when she saw him do that. This led to her feeling angry, and it was her husband's turning on the television that became the trigger for her anger.

***Stage Two:* Threat** (you feel afraid that you will lose something you value)

You next determine that there is danger, that this person's actions are a threat to your body, your property, your freedom, or your self-esteem. You feel afraid that you will lose your safety, your possessions, your power, or his love and approval.

■ **A threat to your body means physical hurt, loss of safety...**

If you are beaten, stabbed, or shot, it is obvious that you are being physically hurt and may lose your life. There is a real threat in such a situation. However, you could you feel just as threatened if someone you know slapped you on the back as a greeting. It would be an uninvited touch and you might be afraid of getting hurt. If the person were a stranger and not a friend, it could seem even more scary.

■ **A threat to your property means loss of possessions...**

If your house is robbed, your car is stolen, or your pocket is picked, you really lose something you own. However, you may experience the same sense of loss and invasion of your property if a friend does not return a book he borrowed from you or if he uses something of yours without asking you first. Your anger in the latter situation may be just as strong as in the former ones.

■ **A threat to your freedom means loss of power...**

If you are kidnapped and tied up, you have your freedom taken away. However, you may feel that same loss of power and feel angry if you are in any of the following situations.

Check off all those that make you angry:

☐ being asked personal questions
☐ being told what to do
☐ feeling trapped in a situation
☐ having someone put his face very close when talking to me
☐ having someone make demands on my time
☐ having someone overly concerned about me
☐ being dependent on someone for care or money

■ **A threat to your self-esteem means emotional hurt and loss of love and approval...**

If you are like most people, you are more often angry about the loss of love and approval than about any other issue, and more often think your self-esteem is being threatened than is your body, your property, or your freedom. You can think you have been emotionally hurt whenever someone disappoints you, rejects you, betrays or deceives you, criticizes you, takes you for granted, ignores you, or is disrespectful to you.

Nancy thought that Joe's being focused on the television while she was with him meant she had lost his love and she was afraid that she would be hurt by Joe again.

You can think you have lost someone's love or approval and be wrong about it, especially if he doesn't even know you. If a waiter is slow in serving you, is he really rejecting you or being disrespectful? Is he attacking your self-esteem? Maybe he is new on the job or just not efficient.

Stage Three: **Blame and Intent** (you feel wronged, blame this person for intending to hurt you)

Anger is about holding someone responsible for wronging you. To feel angry, you must have someone to blame. You must be angry at someone. That means you make the assumption that he is purposely trying to hurt you or means to ignore you. It does not matter what his intentions really are, only what you believe them to be.

Up to this point, Nancy's thoughts were causing her to feel attacked, threatened, worried, and hurt. Now, she decided that her husband wanted to make her feel bad. She believed he had no interest in her and assumed that he turned on the television in order to hurt her.

It turned out that Nancy often talked to Joe about her unhappiness at work, and this gave Joe a lot of anxiety. He then turned on the television to tune Nancy out and protect himself from feeling anxious, not in order to hurt her.

When you feel angry in some situations, it may not be clear who you can blame. There is no question about the intentions of a person who beats or robs you, but more often you are faced with someone whose motivation is less obvious.

You may say you are angry at your car for breaking down, but your anger would imply that you believe the car has chosen to break down. You can say it is unfair that you cannot afford a new car and be angry because you think you deserve to have one. You can say you blame fate for your being in the situation, but it is more likely that you blame a real person, such as one of your parents.

You can feel angry if a friend makes a negative comment about your tie and you believe he is doing it to hurt you. You probably won't feel angry if a very young child makes similar comments and you think he means no harm.

You can feel angry if a friend is late for an appointment with you and you think it shows he doesn't care about you. If you find out he is late because his car would not start, then you know his lateness has nothing to do with his feelings about you.

If you don't take the time to question people about their actions, you can easily assume the worse, feel hurt, and then blame them for hurting you.

Stage Four: **Disappointment** (you feel sad that he has not lived up to your expectations)

At this stage, you may see that someone is trying to hurt you, and if it is a surprise to you because you expected different behavior from him, you will probably be disappointed. That means you feel a form of sadness, but still not anger.

Now that Nancy assumed her husband was meaning to hurt her, she measured his actions against her expectations. She thought he would always treat her well and now she saw he had let her down.

When someone mistreats you, it doesn't have much impact on you if that is what you expect him to do since he has many times before. When you don't feel surprised or disappointed, you may not become angry.

Stage Five: **Anger at Your Attacker** (you object to being mistreated by him)

After you blame someone for purposely being hurtful, you can choose to ignore what he did, you can run away, or you can blame yourself. If you do, you are giving in to his actions and to your fear. If you choose to stay and protest, you become angry with him. You may or may not want to voice those objections.

Nancy objected to having her husband shut her out. She wanted his undivided attention and became angry when she did not get it. She did not tell him she was angry because she was afraid he would become explosive and out of control. He had a tendency to do that any time he thought he was being criticized.

If Nancy had told her husband how she felt, she could have found out that her assumptions about him were not accurate. His actions were about his anxiety and not about lack of love for Nancy.

or....Anger at Yourself (you think it is your fault)

You may believe someone means to hurt you, but you may think you deserve it and that you are to blame for it. Then, you get angry with yourself instead of with him. Sometimes, you may do this because you want to avoid confronting him, and if you blame yourself, you don't have to. Unfortunately, getting angry with yourself can lower your self-image.

Your Anger and Your Thoughts

What good is knowing how your anger happens? It helps you realize that you have control over whether or not you get angry in any situation, how angry you get, and how long you stay angry.

The whole process of getting angry may only take a few seconds or a few minutes, and it can happen automatically without your awareness of it. However, all along the way, you have an inner dialog of thoughts, perceptions, beliefs, and feelings. At any point, you have the ability to interrupt these thoughts and question their validity. You can ask yourself why people seem to be mistreating you, if you should take it personally or if their reasons really have nothing to do with you. When you can do that, you can stop yourself from becoming angry.

To see how this process of becoming angry works, imagine yourself in the following situation: You are driving very slowly on an icy, narrow road in a no-passing zone.

- **The trigger:** Suddenly, a driver comes behind you and starts to tailgate.

- **The threat and fear of loss:** You see that he might hit your car because he is so close, so his actions threaten your safety. You are afraid of getting hurt or having the car damaged. You can decide to speed up or try to pull to the right and let him pass. If you stay with your fear at this point, or if you view this driver as very foolish, you will not be angry. Instead, you will probably choose to get out of his way.

- **Blame:** You may believe he is out to get you, that he wants to hit you because you are going slowly. You then blame him for trying to endanger your safety.

- **Anger:** You get angry at the driver for trying to tell you to go faster. You may want to pay him back by slowing down even more, which can more easily result in his hitting you. If he gets angry at this point, he may hit you on purpose. If, however, you are used to blaming yourself, you may understand why this driver is annoyed, agree that he should want you to go faster, and then you may speed up.

As you can see, what you tell yourself about a situation leads to your feelings about it. Try to pay attention to your thoughts as you interact with others. Remember that every time you feel angry, there are accompanying thoughts. You are more in charge of your anger when you know what you are thinking.

2. IDENTIFYING YOUR ANGER

Identifying Anger Signals

How can you know when you feel angry? All you have to do is pay attention to the signals sent by your body.

When you feel angry, you think you are being threatened. Your mind then sends your body a message that there is danger. Even if your mind perceives danger when it is not there, your body responds as if it were real. It gets you ready to defend against an enemy. What happens then is you have:

- **a surge of adrenaline...** Your whole system gets speeded up so you can fight.
- **increased energy...** You feel restless, slam doors, pace around the room.
- **a rise in blood pressure...** Your face flushes, feels warm, looks red.
- **a rapid heartbeat...** You worry that someone will hurt you or you will hurt him.
- **agitation...** You are charged up and can't sit still.

If you don't release your anger, these signals may increase. If ever you are not sure what you feel, you can look for these changes in your body and know that you probably are angry. When someone else exhibits these signs, you can assume he is angry even if he denies it.

How Strong Is Your Anger?

The intensity of your anger may vary, and you can tell what it is by your words and your actions in any situation.

You have a **weak to mild** amount of anger if:

- When frustrating or annoying situations occur, such as rude clerks, long lines, or noisy people, you can overlook them or laugh about

them.
- When you do feel angry, it is only for a few minutes.
- Your body stays calm before, during, and after any situation. This is because you don't take things seriously, not because you are in denial about feeling angry.
- You say you feel *frustrated*, *annoyed*, *irritated*, or *resentful*.

You have a **moderate** amount of anger if:
- You can identify it when you feel it and it is gone after you express it.
- What you feel like doing when you are angry is to slightly raise your voice.
- Your body gets somewhat tense but recovers in a short while to a calmer state.
- You say you are *mad* or *pissed*.

You have a **strong** amount of anger if:
- You think you are in grave danger and have to defend yourself.
- It lasts more than a few hours, even as much as several days after something happens.
- It envelops your whole body, you feel charged up, ready to explode, out of control, unable to sit still, to think clearly or to hear what is said to you.
- You want to attack others and even hurt those you love.
- It takes a long time for you to calm down.
- You say you are *furious*, *boiling*, or *enraged*.

On the basis of this description, how intense do you think your anger is in most situations?

☐ weak   ☐ mild   ☐ moderate   ☐ strong   ☐ extreme

Once you determine how strong your anger usually is, you can decide if you want to change it. If it is usually weak, you may want it to become stronger so you can be more aware of feeling it. If it is usually very strong, you may want it to be less because it is too draining. Having anger of moderate intensity is the least problematical.

What Intensifies Your Anger

Have you noticed that at certain times, you feel angry about a situation, and at other times, you don't? That on certain days, you are more angry about everything than on other days? That you are a more angry person than you used to be?

Although you may have a level of anger that is fairly consistent, it is not likely that it is always the same. There are many factors which can lower your tolerance level for frustration and intensify your anger. Some of these are:

■ **Feeling bad about yourself...**

On days when your self-esteem is high, you are probably not bothered by what other people do or say to you. When something traumatic happens, like losing your job, your self-esteem may drop. Then, you can become more sensitive to criticism and take more personally the actions of others. If you want to avoid feeling angry about everything, you have to work on feeling good most of the time.

■ **Being tense and anxious...**

When you are under pressure at work, when you are concerned about losing your job, or when you are anxious about anything else, you may be more irritable with people and less tolerant of their imperfections than at other times. To be angry less easily, you have to reduce the amount of tension in your life. When that is not possible, you can at least let people know that you are going through a rough time and that you may be grouchy as a result.

■ **Being ill or physically uncomfortable...**

When you are tired, are in pain, or are feeling sick, you have less tolerance than at other times for conflict and discomfort; you feel hurt more easily; and you are less able to deal with people without feeling angry.

Your emotions are affected by your body chemistry, by what you eat and drink. If any substances are toxic to your system, you may have an allergic reaction. That can change your disposition, make you irritable and quick to anger.

You may find that you become nervous, jumpy, and angry after you have several cups of coffee throughout a day. You have to see if that does not happen on days when you have less coffee. If caffeine seems to affect you negatively, you could switch to de-caffeinated coffee or stop having any coffee. Any withdrawal symptoms would cease when your body adjusted to the change, and you would be calmer.

Drugs and alcohol affect your brain and cause you to distort reality. After you use them, you may become paranoid and believe people are out to harm you when they are not. You may lose your temper and even become violent. Even if you don't see drugs or alcohol affecting your behavior, it may be apparent to people who know you.

Eating sweets can also make you feel angry more easily. Sugar and simple carbohydrates raise your blood sugar, then drop it to a lower level. That can cause you to view the world negatively, feel depressed, and be overly sensitive to what others are doing so you feel hurt and angry.

Besides reactions to sugar, many people have a problem with wheat, milk, and corn. In fact, any food can become toxic to your system and cause bloating, gas, and irritability. You have to see if eliminating some foods from your diet make you calmer.

Since your eating and your emotions are linked, to be less angry you need to stay away from irritants. You need to eat a lot of vegetables, fruit, and grains, and to provide your nervous system with enough B vitamins, calcium and magnesium. If you think that you are nutritionally deficient, try adding these supplements to your diet, or check with a nutritionist.

■ Caring about someone...

The intensity of your anger is affected by how important someone is to you. You probably get more angry with people who are close to you than with those who mean nothing to you. You may readily accept advice when it is given by a stranger but view it as criticism when it comes from a relative. This is because you don't care what the stranger thinks of you but you want approval from a relative. The more you care what someone thinks, the more sensitive you are to being hurt and angry by what he says.

- **Having a hot temperament...**

You may be high strung, jumpy, and impatient, and have a short fuse, and your sister or brother may be quiet, easy-going, and undemanding. You were born with a way of reacting to your environment and probably have the same temperament now that you had as an infant. You can learn to change it, but it may take a lot of work.

- **Having unresolved past anger...**

Your anger is intensified by the hurts or conflicts you experienced in the distant or recent past, especially when similar situations occur now.

When Todd was a child living in a cramped apartment, he hated it when his parents and sisters screamed at each other. He felt trapped because he could not get away from the noise and lack of privacy. As a result, he grew up to be overly sensitive to loud conversations from people in movie theaters or restaurants, and be angry when he heard them.

Phyllis felt powerless as a child when she could not stop her father from being abusive to her. When her teenage daughter was defiant to her, she was absolutely furious with her.

Phyllis reacted to her daughter with more anger than was necessary because her daughter's abuse gave her the same sense of powerlessness she had felt in her childhood.

Marsha's family was poor, and as a child, she had to wear her older sister's discarded clothes. She hated doing so and was constantly angry. As an adult, she could afford decent clothes, but was jealous of other women who dressed well.

Marsha reacted to other women as though she was confusing them with her sister.

Pete felt hurt and angry as a child about not getting enough attention from his parents. As an adult, he became very angry if he was ignored, especially by a waiter in a restaurant.

Pete was angry about the same unresolved issue that triggered his anger as a child.

Dee was a friendly, outgoing woman who lived in a large city. After her apartment was robbed, she became very guarded with everyone, even her friends. When they came to visit, she would not let them touch anything of hers. If they did, she became furious.

None of these people were really being hurt by slow waiters, loud talkers, well-dressed women, defiant children or people touching their things. They just were overly sensitive when others reminded them of those they had been angry with in the past.

If you still have issues from childhood, there may be a connection between how angry you get now and what you were angry about then.

Complete the following statements:

As a child, I was angry because _____

Now, I get angry when _____

Is there any similarity between what you get angry about now and what made you angry as a child? Did you grow up with a loving, supportive family or were they abusive? Were you praised or frequently criticized? Do you get angry now if people criticize you? Did you have enough privacy? Is lack of privacy an issue you get angry about now? Did you get your share of attention or were you ignored or taken for granted? Are you angry now about lack of attention or approval? Were you teased by other children? Do you get angry now when people tease you?

If you see that you tend to overreact to people's actions because of unresolved issues, you might want to work with a professional counselor. When you can put your past behind you, it is not as likely that you will get angry at people because they remind you of others from that time.

How Frequent Is Your Anger?

The following checklist can help you decide if you are angry too often.

> **Mark off the statements that are true for you:**
> ☐ I feel angry more than a few days a week.
> ☐ At some time every day, I feel angry with someone in my family, on the road,
> at work, or elsewhere.
> ☐ People in my life say I am angry too often.

If all of these statements are true, you are angry too often and may want to change it. The best way to do that is to become aware of what triggers your anger so that you can either avoid the triggers or learn to think differently about them.

What Triggers Your Anger

What you feel threatened about depends entirely on what you see people do and what you think you will lose as a consequence. Certain generalities can be made for everyone:

when people	it is a threat to	you fear loss of
steal, borrow, touch your things	your property	your possessions
touch you, stand close	your body	your safety
boss, manipulate, smother, invade	your freedom	your control
criticize, reject, betray, ignore you	your self-esteem	their love, approval

The following questionnaires are about what triggers your anger. The first two were filled in by people in a group workshop on anger management and lists the answers they gave. The third one is blank and is meant for you to fill in.

The group participants were asked to see if they had people in their lives, like those listed in the first column of the chart, who did things that angered them. They were to write next to those they picked exactly what each one did that triggered their anger, what feelings they had about that, and, in the last column, to say if this was a threat to their body, their property, their freedom, or their self-esteem. They were to leave blank the columns for people who did not make them angry.

The first questionnaire was filled in by a married man of about 50 with a teenage son:

I am angry with	when they	I feel	this threatens my
waiters	bring the wrong dish	misunderstood	self-esteem
clerks	sell defective items	betrayed	self-esteem
cashiers			
drivers	cut me off	not respected	self-esteem
boss	gives me no praise	taken for granted	self-esteem
friends	don't call me	ignored	self-esteem
spouse	shows no affection	unloved	self-esteem
parents	criticize me	rejected	self-esteem
children (son)	doesn't do what I ask	unloved	self-esteem
siblings (sister)	hogs the limelight	ignored	self-esteem
relatives			
politicians			
others			

You can see that this man's anger was related to his fears about not being loved. When someone did something that made him feel ignored, rejected, taken for granted, or not given recognition, his self-esteem was threatened and he was angry.

It may be that this man set himself up for rejection by failing to communicate his needs to others. He never told his friends that he wanted them to call, his wife that he wanted her to be more affectionate, his sister that he wanted her to show more interest in his life, or his son that his lack of cooperation seemed unloving. There was a chance they would have given him what he wanted if they knew how he felt.

The chart of an eighteen year old girl living with her parents and two younger sisters revealed different triggers. She had a boyfriend, and was sensitive about being slightly overweight:

I am angry with	when they	I feel	this threatens my
waiters			
clerks			
cashiers			
drivers	create traffic	trapped	freedom
boss	tells me what to do	helpless	freedom
friends	comment on my eating	invaded	freedom
spouse / boyfriend	makes all decisions	helpless	freedom
parents	ask personal questions	invaded	freedom
children			
siblings (sister)	wear my clothes	invaded	freedom
relatives			
politicians			
others (teachers)	grades me unfairly	picked on	self-esteem

This girl got angry about being in traffic, having her boss tell her what to do, having her boyfriend make all of the decisions, having her sisters wear her clothes without asking, or having her parents invade her privacy because they seemed like threats to her freedom and being in control.

She needed to take more charge of her life and not let others push her around. The more independent she became, the less likely it was that people would tell her what to do, or if they did, that she would feel so angry about it.

What makes you angry is not necessarily the same as it was for these two people.

The next chart has been left blank for you to determine the source of your anger.

Fill in the answers appropriate for your life:

I am angry with	when they	I feel	this threatens m
waiters			
clerks			
cashiers			
drivers			
boss			
friends			
spouse			
parents			
children			
siblings			
relatives			
politicians			
others			

When you finish filling in the questionnaire, look at the last two columns and see if any answer is repeated more than once. If so, you know what you are most likely to take personally.

Whether or not a situation triggers your anger depends on how threatened you feel. When you know what the triggers are, you know what situations to avoid in order to be less angry. Perhaps you see that you mostly get angry about threats to your self-esteem, especially when you think you are being ignored. Knowing that means telling people in your life that you need extra attention, and it means that you need to frequent restaurants and shops with good service and avoid ones that are too busy.

3. FEELING LESS ANGRY AT OTHERS

Consider that:

- It is better to feel angry about being mistreated than to ignore it or blame yourself. The anger makes you take a stand against it and can lead to better treatment.
- It is better to know you are feeling angry than to be out of touch. Then, you are in charge of your anger.
- It is better to feel angry only about important things and not waste your energy on trivial ones. Then, you have less hassles with others and you are calmer.
- It is better to feel a moderate amount of anger and only when you are really being threatened. Then, there is less wear and tear on your body.

Are you too angry? You can have less anger when you change the belief system that triggers that anger. Remember, you cannot change how other people behave, you can only change your thoughts about their actions. That means changing your **expectations** and your **assumptions**.

Changing Your Expectations

Angry feelings are often the result of being disappointed with people because they fail to live up to your expectations. But what if those expectations are unrealistic? If they are, you can be disappointed and angry very frequently.

22

> **Check off the statements that are true for you:**
>
> I expect people (family, boss, clerks, doctors, others) to:
>
> ☐ be what I want them to be (kind, productive, efficient, smart, etc.)
>
> ☐ think the way I think (agree with my opinions, feelings, values)
>
> ☐ change for my benefit (become what I want them to be)
>
> ☐ put my needs first (not theirs)
>
> ☐ treat me the way I treat them (loving, caring)
>
> ☐ reward me for my virtues (with praise, recognition)
>
> ☐ know what I want (without my telling them)
>
> ☐ always be fair

Do you see that you expect people to be a certain way and act according to your needs? If you checked more than half of the items as true for you, than you are setting yourself up for disappointment.

Making Your Expectations Realistic

Many people will not do or be the things you want. If you expect they will, you are not being realistic and are likely to be surprised when most of them behave differently. To be less angry, you need to change your expectations as follows:

■ **Expect people to behave in many different ways...**

It would be great if everyone was kind and generous and well-mannered. Maybe you are and so you think everyone is like you. Of course, there are many people who are admirable, but there are also many others who are lazy, crazy, mean, sloppy, unreliable, or selfish.

Instead of getting upset when you see people with unpleasant behavior, try to avoid having them in your life. Shop only in stores where the salespeople are courteous. Eat only in restaurants where you get good food and service. Hire only contractors who are efficient. Use only the services of people who are polite and reliable. Keep as friends only the people with qualities you admire.

When you don't see very many people measuring up to your standards, you will be less angry about it if that is what you expect.

■ **Expect people to behave according to their culture...**

It is not realistic to think that everyone is going to have the same customs as you. Every culture has its own way of doing things and people are influenced by it.

If you travel to other countries, you can see people with different concepts of time. Some pride themselves on promptness and precision. Others consider it fine to be late for an appointment or take forever to complete a task.

In some countries, people express their anger explosively and think nothing of public displays of temper. They speak when they have something to say, even when it means interrupting someone else. In other countries, people are very formal about addressing each other. They hold back all their emotions and never say they are angry.

Even in your own town, people with a different ethnic background than yours may have a very different way of behaving, depending on their cultural heritage. They may fit into the main culture, but then have other customs that are based on what they were taught by their families.

Rather than judge the behavior of others by your standards, you would be less angry if you viewed them in their cultural context.

■ **Expect people to make mistakes...**

Do you expect everyone to be efficient? Do you get angry with a bank teller if she is slow? with a waitress if she brings the wrong dish? with a checkout clerk if he rings up the wrong price? with the mail carrier if he puts your letter in a neighbor's box? with the news carrier if he doesn't bring your paper? with your answering service if they foul up a message? with someone in your family if he makes mistakes?

Of course these things are annoying and inconvenient, but you can expect them to happen because people are imperfect and make mistakes. They all function on a different level of efficiency and ability. Some are completely organized, but others are unable to be. That is just how it is, no matter how much you want everyone to be infallible.

Instead of being angry with people you love because they make mistakes, give them help if they need it. When dealing with commercial establishments, make the decision to only use those establishments that have employees who are efficient.

■ **Expect people to be unfair...**

Do you get angry about being treated unfairly? Have you been betrayed by anyone? Has someone less qualified than you been given a promotion that you applied for? When you were growing up, did your brother or sister get more attention than you did?

You should get what you deserve, but you may not because life is full of injustice. Many people do not care about being fair, and being bitter about it does not help to change anything. It is better to find people who are fair and keep them in your life. It is more realistic not to expect that everyone will be fair.

If seeing global injustice gets you angry, you would do better to take some kind of action to try to change it. You can write letters of complaint to heads of hotels, banks, governments; you can give money to groups that support your point of view; you can run for some office to promote your ideas. There is no guarantee of change, but at least you can know you tried.

■ **Expect people to care more about themselves than you...**

Cary was the mother of two boys, one ten and one twelve years old. When she cleaned her house, she expected them to volunteer to help her. She felt angry because they never did.

Cary's expectations were unreasonable. It was normal for children their ages to be more focused on their own needs than on hers. Cary needed to accept the fact that the only way to get help from her boys was to tell them she wanted it. Otherwise, she was doomed to being angry.

Certainly, if you are kind and giving to others, you deserve to be thanked. If you are courteous, you deserve to be treated with respect. If you do a good job with something, you deserve to be praised and given recognition.

However, it is unrealistic to think that because you deserve these things, people will give them to you. Many of them are users and takers and will give you nothing. They are only interested in what you can do for them.

Actually, people don't really owe you anything, and you can be angry all of the time if you think they do. You just have to find the people who are interested in you and have as little as possible to do with those who are self-centered.

■ Expect people to behave as they did in the past...

Jan had an aunt who talked very loud and also interrupted her whenever she tried to talk. Every time her aunt came to visit, Jan was annoyed and angry with her. She really expected her aunt to be quieter than she had been other times.

What Jan failed to realize is that her aunt's being loud and abrasive was part of her personality and was unlikely to change. When Jan learned to anticipate her aunt's behavior, she was less angry about it.

Patricia was upset about her recent divorce and called her mother to tell her, expecting her to be supportive. She was angry and disappointed when she was not.

Patricia's expectations were not realistic. She should have known her mother would not treat her well because all through her life, her mother had been wrapped up in her own needs.

Laura was married to a man who periodically beat her. Each time it happened, Laura wanted to leave him. Then, he would become remorseful and promise it would not happen again. Laura would believe him and stay, and then he would repeat the abuse.

Laura needed to get out of her marriage. When someone's behavior is destructive, it is unrealistic to think he is going to change. If he has always been abusive, has lied or betrayed your trust, he is likely to do it again. People don't usually change unless they have counseling, and maybe not even then.

When you know how someone has behaved in the past, you know what to expect in the future. Each person lives according to his own script of behavior and so he becomes a stereotype. When you watched Archie Bunker on television, you knew what he was going to say or do in any given situation. You laughed when he then did it. He was consistent and predictable, the way most people are in real life.

If you expect someone to be annoying because he always has been, you won't be surprised and disappointed when he is.

Making No Assumptions

When you assume the actions of others are meant to be hurtful, you take what they do personally. The following stories illustrate the ways many people can misinterpret the motivations of others:

A young woman named Ann could not afford to hire a sitter for her baby while she went to work. She was grateful that her mother-in-law was willing to be the sitter. However, every time she came, she criticized everything Ann was doing with her baby, and told her how she thought it should be done. Ann assumed that her mother-in-law considered her to be a poor mother.

Why it's not personal: Ann was wrong about why her mother-in-law criticized her. It was to make her feel inadequate, in the hope that Ann would be dependent on her. She was afraid that unless Ann needed her, Ann would have nothing to do with her.

Ann needed to tell her mother-in-law that she appreciated her helping but not her being controlling. For Ann to do that, she had to get beyond feeling hurt and angry. She had to understand that her mother-in-law's behavior was about herself and not really about Ann. If her mother-in-law felt more welcome, she might have been less critical.

A man and woman who had been married for twenty years were taking a car trip to a popular tourist area. The man was driving, and while he was looking for their hotel, he got out the wrong exit on the highway. When his wife mentioned it to him, he got angry and yelled at her.

Many times throughout the marriage, he had reacted with anger to her making any reference to a mistake he made. Each time, she felt crushed because she assumed that if he was angry with her, he must not care about her.

Why it's not personal: Actually, the man was not yelling at his wife because he disliked her or even because of what she said. What happened was that he knew she had seen him make a mistake, he was disappointed in himself and assumed she must be too. He was yelling in anticipation of her disapproval, whether he got it from her or not. She was very important to him and he wanted her approval.

The woman did not really think less of her husband when he made a mistake. She assumed that pointing it out would help him correct it. When she was able to stop taking his anger so personally, she was able to tell him what her motives were.

Clara went to an informal club meeting as the guest of one of the members. At the meeting, Clara was angry when the other members ignored her and seemed more interested in what a rather bossy woman named Lois had to say. Clara assumed the women in the club didn't like her.

Why it's not personal: It was not true that the women in the club had no interest in Clara. They just had no chance to talk to her because they felt intimidated by Lois and allowed her to dominate each meeting.

When you observe someone's actions, you have no way of knowing what he means unless you ask him. You could make the assumption that he is trying to hurt you and so be angry, but you could be wrong. Your anger could be a waste of energy, and could result in your unfairly accusing someone. Making negative assumptions could make you needlessly unhappy.

Check off what you usually assume in the following situations:

In a restaurant, a waiter brings you milk for your coffee when you asked for cream. This means:

☐ He doesn't like my face.

☐ He has a poor memory and often makes mistakes with orders.

On the road, you get cut off by a driver. This means:

☐ He doesn't like me.

☐ He is an aggressive person with no regard for others.

At a family gathering, your mother criticizes you. This means:

☐ She thinks I am a failure.

☐ She cannot accept her own imperfections or mine.

☐ She needs to control me to feel important.

The child next door runs away when he sees you. This means:

☐ He thinks I am awful.   ☐ He is shy.

At work, your boss challenges every decision you make. This means:

☐ He thinks I am a failure.   ☐ He is threatened by my competency.

What do your answers seem to indicate? In most situations, do you assume people have a low opinion of you or they want to hurt you? Do you wait to see what motivates them? When you do that, you may find out that what they are doing has nothing to do with you.

What You Believe, You Will Perceive

The expectations you have about people and the assumptions you make about them influence the way you react to what they do.

If you believe that people like you, you expect them to treat you well. You then interpret their actions as friendly or at least neutral. Even when they are sometimes critical, you are able to overlook it.

If you believe that people are against you, you expect them to hurt you. You then ignore anything loving or supportive that they do, and you interpret their actions as an intended threat to your freedom or your self-esteem. You have your radar out for their hostility, and because you look for it, you find it. If you go to a party, you are sure everyone is noticing that you are overweight. If a friend says he is too tired to go to the movies with you, you are sure it is because he doesn't want to be with you.

When you make negative assumptions that people are out to get you, you are saying that they have nothing better to do than to focus on you. How can it be that everything they say or do is with you in mind? How can their every move be planned ahead of time in such a way as to upset you?

The fact is that people are too busy with their own needs to be that interested in you. In fact, when they are with you, their main interest is probably to see if you are noticing them. Most people are not out to hurt you, just to prevent you from hurting them. When you accept that idea, you give up some sense of your own importance.

The only time you can know for certain that someone has in mind to harm you in some way is if he tells you so, or if you know that he is treating everyone else better than he is treating you. Otherwise, you know that you have not been singled out and whatever he is doing is more about him than it is about you.

Before You Get Mad

When people do things that begin to trigger your anger, you can ward it off if you first ask yourself these questions:

■ **Why is this person behaving this way?**

In any situation, try to see where the other person is coming from before you jump to conclusions. It is hardly ever true that someone's behavior reflects his intention to hurt you. It is almost always true that it just tells you something about him, not you. This applies to people close to you, as well as to strangers.

Try to find out what is going on with him, where he is coming from. If you can't ask him, just give him the benefit of the doubt before you assume his motivation has anything to do with you.

■ **Am I really being threatened?**

Before you assume your body, your property, your freedom or especially your self-esteem are being threatened by someone, take a long look at what his actions are really about. Since it is hardly ever true that people really want to attack others, you will probably find your perception of danger is not accurate.

■ **Are my expectations realistic?**

See if you are expecting this person to behave in a way that he cannot because of his age, his level of ability, his lack of experience, or his emotional problems. If you are, your unrealistic expectations can lead to feeling disappointed and angry.

■ **What can I do about this situation?**

Some situations are beyond your control and have to be accepted. You can't make the weather better; you can't end the traffic; you can't make your children grow up any faster; you can't stop your baby from getting ill; you can't make someone competent who is not. Getting angry serves no purpose.

Most things that happen are temporary anyway, so if you wait it out and do nothing, they end by themselves. Bad weather clears; you get out of traffic; sickness, pain, and financial problems improve; unruly children become responsible adults; your baby stops crying; new and more skilled people come to replace those who are not.

When you see that a situation can be changed, take action to improve it. End a destructive relationship, leave a job you hate, move away from an invasive family, walk out of a restaurant where the service is poor, and replace a car that keeps breaking down. When you take charge of your life, you cease being a victim and you feel much less angry.

■ **Am I partly to blame?**

Take time to consider whether you are at least partly responsible for how someone is behaving. You can be angry when your teenage son acts rebellious and uncooperative. However, you may be giving him too many rules, and he may be reacting in the only way he can. If so, working out a compromise with him is better than yelling at him.

You can be angry when your boss criticizes your work. However, you may really be doing sloppy work or not asking for help when you need it. Maybe your making some changes will lead him to treat you better.

You can be angry when a clerk in a store is rude to you after you ask her for information. However, it may be that you spoke in a nasty way and she feels attacked. You need to look at what your tone of voice usually conveys to people.

■ **Is this worth being angry about?**

Something that happens may seem very important to you: a driver cutting in front of you; a mechanic overcharging you; your son dropping his clothes on the floor or answering you back when you scold him. Should you waste your energy getting angry about situations that are really trivial? Should you get upset about people who mean nothing to you? Should you be destructive to people who do matter to you? Will ignoring any of them spoil anything for you?

Most things that happen are not worth your getting upset. Ask yourself if any situation is important enough for you to scream and yell, have your heart race, become frazzled and upset others? Does it matter that much?

Try to let unimportant issues go without reacting negatively to them. Learn to say "so what" or to remove yourself if possible. If you wait before you express your anger, you will see that the passage of time will automatically soften your angry feelings. If you can become detached, you will be calmer and less angry.

4. FEELING LESS ANGRY AT HOME

Living with Someone

Whenever you deal with people, you see them do things that can trigger your anger. Most of them are probably strangers, but even friends and relatives can let you down or be annoying.

Fortunately, your interaction with most of these people is usually brief and temporary. You certainly do not have to do business with those service people who are unsatisfactory, so you can get them out of your life. You do not have to see friends or relatives who irritate you any more often than you choose.

You don't have that option when you live with someone. Even if you are both sensible, stable people with good self-images, all sorts of issues about time, space, money, and love are likely to come up and lead to conflict, competition, and hurt feelings. No matter whether this person is your lover, friend, spouse, child, parent, or roommate, you are probably going to be angry more often if you live with him than if you only know him outside of your home.

There are several reasons why living with someone can trigger your anger:

■ **You are with him constantly....**

When you live under the same roof with someone, you live with all of his personality traits, his habits, needs, defenses, fears, quirks, distortions, interests, values, morals, opinions, and religious views. You live with how much noise he makes, when he goes to bed or gets up, how long it takes him to do things, how social he is, how much energy he has, how seriously he takes life, how much he worries, how much he likes to be involved in activities, and how he expresses his feelings. If something he does gets on your nerves, you can't really get away from it.

■ **He invades your space...**

When you live with someone, he is probably with you most of the time and can see everything you do. It is hard under those circumstances to have any privacy, to keep any secrets from him. There is also the possibility that he will open your mail or look through your belongings when you are not there, or ask you too many personal questions.

Since you and the person you live with use the same rooms, appliances, television set, furniture, closets, shower, and maybe the phone, there may be conflicts about his wanting to use them at the same time as you.

■ **He makes demands...**

Unless the person you live with is rather complaisant, he probably won't always let you do what you want. He may tell you which television show to watch, how hot or cold the room should be, how to decorate the room, and, if you share finances, what to do with your money. He may talk to you when you are busy; may make demands on your time that sometimes conflict with what you want to do; and may want to go places with you when you have other ideas.

■ **He brings his past...**

Whoever you live with brings into the relationship his feelings about all of the people he has ever known. They helped make him what he is, which may mean trouble for you. If he was abused, he may be insecure and frightened and want constant attention from you, or he may be hostile and rude and shut you out. If he was overindulged, he may be immature, demanding, and self-centered. If he was brought up strictly, he may be rigid and unwilling to compromise on anything.

■ **He takes you for granted...**

When someone sees you all the time, he is likely to take you for granted. He may not be as polite to you as he is to his friends or anyone else he meets. He may not thank you for helping him or for being supportive. He may forget that you have needs.

■ **He lets you down...**

When someone is there all of the time, you have many more opportunities to see how he is treating you than you do with people outside of your home. If he does not measure up, you may be angry with him.

Since he is more accessible to you than other people, it is easy for you to expect him to satisfy all of your needs. You may become possessive and feel hurt if he pays attention to anyone else. You may want him to go everywhere and do everything with you and be disappointed if he doesn't want to.

■ **He tries to change you...**

No matter who you live with or what the relationship is, you may find he dislikes some of your habits or ideas and wants to change them.

Many people purposely choose to live with someone in a love relationship who is very different from themselves in order to balance their own shortcomings. If they are shy, they don't want someone who also is, so they look for someone who is outgoing. If they are talkative, they want someone who is quiet.

Unfortunately, many people then spend every minute trying to make that other person become a clone of themselves. If he does change, they are happy until he exhibits any traits they don't like in themselves. A disorganized man may find a woman who is neat, try to make her loosen up, but then get angry if he sees her begin to lose things.

If someone tries to change you to be more like him, he is asking you to give up the very traits he originally valued in you. If you do change because he wants you to, you will probably resent him.

The following couples created conflict in their marriage because they could not fully accept each other as they were:

Marshall was a shy, quiet man who enjoyed staying home and reading technical books. He was good at facts and details, but not feelings, and usually felt uncomfortable with people. He was thrilled to meet Elinor because she loved to try new things, was outgoing and friendly, loved concerts, plays and movies, and seemed to pull him out of his shell. She introduced him to a world he had never known.

Elinor had always enjoyed being able to show Marshall new things, and his admiration made her feel good. She needed his quiet ways to balance her enthusiasm and ground her.

After a while, however, Elinor felt inhibited when she was with Marshall and wished he would loosen up more. Marshall wished Elinor would not drag him to so many parties and that she wouldn't talk so much.

Hilda was obsessed with order. She straightened pictures on the wall, lined her shoes up in the closet, and was extremely efficient and clean. Hank was just the opposite. His desk was a mess, he dropped his clothes on the floor, and was always misplacing things.

Hilda was attracted to Hank's laid-back attitude. She envied the way he could be comfortable with chaos, when she could not. Hank was attracted to Hilda's ability to be in charge of her life. He needed someone who could help him be more organized.

In time, however, Hilda couldn't stand Hank's sloppiness, and began to impose her standards on him. He became annoyed with Hilda's rigidity. What he first saw as efficient began to seem uptight.

Martin was loud, aggressive, and demanding. Fran was very quiet and allowed others to take charge.

Fran was attracted to Martin's ability to stop others from pushing him around. Martin was attracted to Fran's lack of competitiveness, her quiet manner, and her willingness to let him dominate.

In time, however, Martin became bored with Fran's passivity, and Fran was embarrassed by Martin's loudness in public. She resented his making decisions for her and thought him invasive and abrasive.

Samantha had a hard time expressing feelings. Her father had abused her and she didn't trust men enough to let them get too close. Justin was used to a lot of attention because as a child, his parents fussed over him, and as an adult, women chased him.

Samantha was attracted to Justin because he was affectionate and he did not try to hurt her. Justin was attracted to Samantha because she was aloof and did not run after him.

In time, however, Samantha saw that Justin had an insatiable need for attention and wished he would leave her alone. Justin wanted Samantha to be more affectionate and became angry that she was not.

Stewart was an optimist who always believed things would work out. He was a free-lance writer and preferred his independence to earning more money in a full time job. Roberta was shy in social settings and had no confidence in her ability to make it in the world alone, either financially or socially.

Stewart was attracted to Roberta because she was more practical and more grounded than him. Roberta saw Stewart as someone on whom she could be emotionally and financially dependent.

In time, Roberta came to consider Stewart a dreamer and saw his disinterest in money as meaning that he didn't care about her or her needs. She felt disappointed in him, depressed, frightened, and angry. Stewart became angry with Roberta for trying to change him and for being such a worrier.

You can see that each person wanted his partner to be a mirror image of himself and to be less the way that person was when they met. Vivacious Elinor wanted shy Marshall to be more outgoing, and he wanted her to be more restrained. Neat Hilda wanted sloppy Hank to be neater, and he wanted her to be less efficient. Passive Fran wanted aggressive Martin to be quieter and he wanted her to be less passive. Needy Justin wanted distant Samantha to be affectionate and she wanted him to be more distant. Practical Roberta wanted carefree Stewart to be more serious, and he wanted her to be freer.

Making It Work

All this doesn't mean you can never live with anyone. It just means that when you do, you have to work hard to make the relationship productive, especially if you care about each other. It helps if you can:

■ **Appreciate him as he is...**

To save their marriage, all of these couples had to become more aware of what they appreciated about each other. They had to stop trying to change the other person. Roberta had to realize that Stewart functioned differently than her. She was a worrier and needed his more carefree attitude. When she stopped seeing herself as so helpless, she was less threatened by his independence. At the same time, Stewart acknowledged that he was glad Roberta was more realistic about things than he was.

What kind of person do you live with? Are you angry with him for being like you or for being very different? Does his behavior annoy you? Are you intolerant of his faults?

The only way to live in peace with someone is by letting him be what he is. It is easier if his interests, values and outlook on life are similar to yours, but they may not be. If you cannot accept his habits or beliefs and always feel angry with him, it would probably be better not to live together.

■ **Accept him with his past hurts...**

Marion and Dennis were in their thirties and had been married for a year. Dennis believed that a wife should stay home with her husband, but Marion liked to go out with her friends. Dennis complained that Marion acted like she was still single.

Marion was angry that Dennis never wanted to go places with her, so she went without him. Any time he asked her to stay home or asked when she was coming back, she got angry and left. Dennis asked because he missed her when she was gone. He often was too tired from working to go out with Marion, but she refused to wait until he was available.

Marion brought baggage from the past into the relationship. She grew up with a mother who never wanted her to leave the house and who dominated her father. He was passive and said nothing to her mother, but then he took his anger out on Marion. She felt criticized and controlled by both of them, and dealt with it by being rebellious and going off by herself whenever she could.

Marion was angry with Dennis for wanting her home as her mother had. She continued to rebel by frequently leaving the house as she had in childhood. She still had a strong need to be in charge, and was afraid that if she ever let Dennis have his way she would lose her identity.

What Marion didn't realize was that Dennis had very different reasons than her mother had for wanting her to be home. Her mother worried about Marion's safety and could only relax if she kept Marion home. She also felt more important when she was controlling her. Dennis felt unloved when Marion went out. He grew up in an unsupportive family and was alone a lot. He despised the isolation and still could not deal with it.

Dennis was taught not to display his emotions, so Marion never knew what he felt. When he felt hurt, he got angry and talked down to her. He needed to become more affectionate, and also to develop some interests of his own to be less dependent. Marion had to feel less threatened when he asked her to be with him. With the help of counseling, Marion and Dennis did get beyond their past hurts and learned to trust each other.

■ **Set boundaries...**

The only way you won't hate someone you live with is by establishing clear rules about living together. You have to tell him what you need, what you don't like, and what you are willing to do. If you bought the exercise bike for yourself, you shouldn't have to wait your turn to use it. If he blasts the stereo when you are trying to rest or read, you have a right to tell him to turn it down.

You can put a lock on the door to your work or sleep area and insist that he knock before entering. You can also refuse to answer personal questions. When you are firm, you get more of what you want and are less angry.

■ **Be willing to compromise...**

If you are arrogant and bossy and always want your own way, the other person may fight back or feel intimidated and pull away. If you are willing to compromise, you show you respect him and there is no need for a power struggle.

■ **Become more separate...**

When you develop your own friends and your own interests, you become less dependent on the person you live with. You can relate in a more balanced way and not be angry if he is ever unavailable.

Just making these changes can mean you are less angry and your relationships can stay in tact.

Living with A Child

When you live with a child of any age, you can expect your anger to be triggered fairly often. This is because of the nature of most children, especially when they are very young:

• A child **demands** your attention, affection, time, and material things. He wants you to be with him at all times and not go to the bathroom or talk on the phone. He wants every toy he sees and gets mad if you say no. The younger he is, the more true this is.

- A child almost completely **depends** on you financially and emotionally. This keeps him tied to you and at times you may consider him a burden.

- A child **invades** your privacy and has no sense of boundaries of where he ends and you begin. He barges into your bedroom, interrupts you when you speak, follows you everywhere, and does not acknowledge your existence as separate.

- A child **wears you out** because he is energetic with few fears. He is forever climbing, running and exploring. You constantly have to run after him to see that he doesn't hurt himself.

- A child has no inhibitions and **is uncivilized**. He may damage your property or say embarrassing things. He puts no boundaries between you and himself.

- A child **makes noise** and has annoying habits. He lacks the controls to stop himself.

- A child **makes a mess**, is unconcerned with neatness, is clumsy and spills things.

- A child is **curious** and asks a lot of annoying questions. He expects you to answer him.

- A child **takes you for granted**, never thanks you for what you do.

- At various ages, a child **refuses to cooperate**, is rude and quarrelsome.

- A child **cries easily** because he is extremely sensitive, feels hurt or frustrated quickly.

- A child **cannot wait** or do without, especially if he is very young. His low tolerance for frustration makes him angry.

- A child **compares and competes** with siblings and peers because he is insecure.

It can be pretty hard to put up with all of these things without feeling impatient, unless you know what to expect.

Making It Work

Luckily, most children become more civilized as time goes on and eventually outgrow these behaviors. How can you be less angry in the meantime? Only by making an effort to do the following:

- **Be realistic** about what is appropriate for his age. Don't expect a very young child to sit still for long periods of time. Don't expect him to behave like an adult. A child won't usually ask you how you are, how your day was, how you feel. He won't usually put your needs above his. If you expect him to, you may be very disappointed and angry.

- **Let him share in making decisions** whenever possible, no matter what his age. If he is very young, give him multiple choices. Ask him if he prefers this to that, rather than an open-ended question of what he wants. No child is too young to say that he has had enough to eat or that he is tired. This doesn't mean he rules the household, but he can certainly make decisions about his own body.

- **Avoid criticizing him**, and give him hugs instead.

- **Set clear boundaries** on what you will do. Say no when you feel like it. Teach him that you have a separate life of your own.

- **Listen to what he is saying**. Try to hear the feelings beneath his words, since he may not be able to communicate clearly.

- Try to **show no preferences** between him and his siblings. Encourage him to compete only with himself and not with his siblings or his peers.

- **Let him make mistakes** without berating or teasing him about them. Try to understand the difference between setting high standards and expecting too much. Don't demand perfection. If you do, he will get frustrated and you will be disappointed.

- **Let him express negative feelings** without being punished, as long as he is respectful to you. You create problems for yourself if you take personally everything he says about you. Most of the time, a child does not mean what he says when he vents anger at a parent.

- **Communicate your feelings** without attacking him. Tell him what bothers you about his behavior.

- **Delegate responsibilities** to him so you are not a slave. Small children love to help out, and older ones will if you get them in the habit of helping at an early age.

- **Welcome differences in each child**, instead of hoping for a clone of you. He may take longer to do things or not be as athletic, but that is what makes him who he is.
- **Maintain a sense of humor** when disruptive things happen. That is more effective than yelling.
- **Hire sitters and leave** when you can. A young child quickly adjusts to being left with someone if he has to do it frequently.

Following these suggestions will help you have a more peaceful time with your child. Although there are a lot of items listed, many of them can be accomplished simply by giving your child the same respect that you want for yourself.

Part Two

EXPRESSING ANGRY FEELINGS

This section discusses the ways you can express your angry feelings:

■ **You can completely hide your anger and be passive...**

If you think you cannot stand up to people who are hurtful, you may try to rationalize away your angry feelings, try to please everyone, or turn the anger on yourself. Instead of expressing your anger openly, you may smile, cry, or go off somewhere by yourself and sulk. Keeping your anger hidden can lead to depression or frequent illness.

■ **You can partly hide your anger and be passive-aggressive...**

If you don't want people to know you are angry, you may express your anger through annoying behavior or manipulation.

■ **You can openly show your anger and be aggressive...**

If you are afraid of being rejected by people, of being attacked by them, or of being smothered by them, you may express your anger with insults, criticism, and intimidation.

■ **You can openly show your anger and be assertive...**

If you see yourself as equal in power to others and are not afraid to confront them, you can express your anger and demand to be treated better without attacking anyone.

5. EXPRESSING ANGER WITHOUT FEAR

When to Keep Quiet

When you feel angry with someone, you may or may not want to express that anger. Under certain conditions, such as the following, it actually would be much better to keep it to yourself:

■ **When someone may be violent...**

Any time you feel angry with someone you don't know very well, you have no way of knowing what is his potential for violence. If there is any possibility he may retaliate, it may not be safe to unleash your anger.

Suppose, for example, that you are walking on the street and a mugger tries to grab your wallet. If you resist by pulling away from him or pushing him, there is a chance that he may hit you or he may have a gun or a knife and use it on you.

Suppose you are driving on a road and at an intersection, another driver cuts across you without signaling. If you furiously blow the horn at him, he may get mad and try to damage your car, or he may get out of his car and punch you.

Suppose someone you are in a relationship with has a bad temper and gets violent when he is angry. If you scream at him when he is raging, he may get more out of control and hurt you.

Your chances of winning a fight against a violent person are very slim. If you keep quiet, you lose nothing except getting the last word. It is best to wait until an enraged person is calm before you stand up to him. It is best to drive away from a rude driver, or to give a mugger what he wants instead of fighting him and then call the police when he leaves.

■ **When someone is out of touch...**

Someone who is emotionally disturbed, severely retarded, or senile will know from your tone of voice that you are angry if you yell at him, but he may not understand the reason. If someone is drunk or on drugs, he may be so out of touch that he cannot even hear what you say when you express your anger to him. If you are dealing with someone whose condition is temporary, you can wait to talk to him. If it is permanent, it would be better to let it go.

■ **When you stand to lose too much...**

Before you express your anger, you have to consider what the consequences of doing so may be. A boss who is reasonable can accept your telling him that you are angry about something, but if he is not, he might fire you. If you create a scene in a restaurant or any other public place by yelling at someone, you may be asked to leave and later feel embarrassed about it. If you constantly express anger to someone you live with, you may destroy the relationship. You have to decide whether any satisfaction you derive from releasing your anger outweighs what you may lose.

Who Sees Your Anger?

Do you express anger to everyone or only to certain people? Are you afraid to express it to others? Who are those people? Who you show your anger to may depend on what you tell yourself about each person and how much you care what they think of you.

Fill in the statements about what you usually do and why.

express my anger to _____ because _____

find it hard to express anger to_____because_____

When a group of people in an anger management workshop filled in this questionnaire, they said different things and had different reasons for their answers:

Anne said she was able to express her anger to her family and friends because she believed they would be supportive no matter what she did. She said nothing to anyone else because she was afraid they would reject her.

Alan could express anger to clerks, waiters, contractors, or other strangers because he didn't care what they thought of him. He did not show his anger to his family because he wanted their approval and was afraid they would reject him.

Peter could express anger to friends, family, and to most people at work because he felt comfortable with them. He could not express it to doctors, teachers, administrators, or lawyers because he regarded them as authority figures and was too in awe of them. He assumed that because they had attended special schools and passed special exams they were wiser than him and more important.

As you can see, Ann, Alan, and Peter each had a completely different rationale for who to confront with their anger. Ann and Alan expressed anger when they felt safe with someone. Peter expressed anger when he felt equal to someone.

Anne and Alan failed to realize that it was their right to protest to anyone who mistreated them. Peter failed to realize that no one in authority was superior to him, or necessarily more competent.

What about you? Do you put people with degrees or titles up on pedestals and feel unequal to them? Does this prevent you from being assertive with them? Do you give people in authority a lot of power?

The fact is that they are all human, just like you, and can make errors, have poor judgment, or be incompetent. When you realize that, you can express anger to anyone.

Ways to Hide Anger

When you are not afraid to tell someone you are angry with him, but you determine it would be better not to, you keep quiet by choice. When you keep quiet because you are afraid of what might happen otherwise, you are ruled by your fear. That means you are not able to say anything, even when you think it is a good idea.

When you feel angry and are afraid to express it, you may try to do the following to cover up the anger:

■ **Smile and act pleasant...**

When people are abusive to you, do you feel angry about it? Do you express the anger, or do you smile and act like you don't mind? Do you really feel that way, or do you think you are supposed to be agreeable at all times?

It is phony to smile when you really feel angry. Wouldn't you have more respect for yourself if you could openly express your anger?

Do you know anyone who never seems angry, no matter what the situation? Is he just a very accepting person, or could his agreeable manner sometimes be a cover for anger? If you found out that it is, would you mind? You cannot always take people at face value because they may not be what they seem.

■ **Leave the room or the situation...**

When you are in the middle of an argument with someone, do you ever go out of the room if that person begins to rant and rave? Do you prefer to wait until he calms down before confronting him with your anger?

It may be that you leave the room when you are angry because you are afraid to have others see you angry. That would be a good idea if it meant the end of your anger. Unfortunately, not expressing it can often make it stay with you for a long time, and it can interfere with your functioning throughout the day.

What happens when you are angry at a close friend? Do you tell him, or do you stop calling him so you won't have to confront him? If he happened to invite you to a party, would you make up an excuse and stay home? If you are angry at your boss or at another employee, do you ever call in sick to avoid facing him? Do you go so far as to think about changing jobs?

You will always meet someone who triggers your anger. If you keep running away when that happens, you can end up eliminating everyone. When you stay around and say what you want, you are more likely to get it.

Does anyone you know run away when he is angry? Is it difficult to be in a relationship with him? It can be if he does not stay around long enough for you to tell him what he does that bothers you.

■ **Show no emotion...**

When most people are angry, their faces get red, they glare at you, they talk loudly, they challenge what you say, they say insulting things, and even throw things or hit you. But some angry people are silent, cold and distant. They hold back their emotions as a way to hurt others or upset them, so their silence can be considered an expression of anger.

When Frank, 39, visited his father, he hardly spoke to him. He told him nothing about recent events in his life, even when he was excited about them. In fact, he gave no response to anything his father said.

Frank was angry at his father because he tended to criticize Frank in front of other people, and because he was very self-centered. His father acted in local theater groups, and whenever Frank came to see him, he spent most of the time showing Frank newspaper reviews that praised his performance. Frank refused to show his father that he was impressed or proud of him. This made his father feel ignored and shut out. As a result, he became hostile to Frank when he got no response.

Frank had made a choice to hold back his anger, his hurt, and even his joy. It prevented him from getting any support from his father. It also led to his feeling dead inside. Once he turned off his emotions, it was difficult for Frank to turn them back on. This made being with other people awkward.

In counseling, Frank had to get in touch with his anger at his father. He had to feel safe enough in the sessions to allow the anger to surface. Once he did that, he felt braver about asserting himself with his father and told him to stop being so critical. He also realized that he was important to his father, who really wanted his support and attention.

In time, Frank expressed more feelings to his father, and talked about himself without waiting for his father to ask him anything. His father became less angry and more caring, and Frank had more self-respect and became more open with other people.

Whenever Peg, 35, went to see her widowed mother in her apartment, she never knew what to expect. Usually, her mother would sit stiffly in a chair, not moving a muscle, her face like a mask, with no expression on it. Sometimes, while Peg was talking to her, she would get up and leave the room without saying a word. Then, she would not call Peg for months.

Peg had no idea what caused her mother to react this way. She guessed that her mother was angry about something that Peg had said, but she had no idea what that was.

Peg had married a man as unexpressive as her mother. He left all decisions to her, didn't complain, had no opinions about anything, and always avoided confrontation. Since he never reacted, Peg didn't know what he felt, but she was frustrated and bored with him.

Peg's husband's lack of complaining may seem to indicate that he was never angry, but that is unlikely. He did not display or express other emotions either, so it can be assumed that feelings were scary to him and he had turned them all off.

Do you keep your anger so well hidden that no one ever knows you are angry? Like Frank, Peg's husband or her mother, you may act cool and unemotional but be boiling inside. When you are afraid to express anything unpleasant, you may stop expressing all feelings and come across as flat and lifeless.

■ **Apologize for being angry...**

When you feel angry about something, do you mildly complain and then apologize for being negative? Do you think it is improper to admit that you are angry? You may not even realize you do this. Try to pay attention the next time you express anger and see if your statement is prefaced with an "I'm sorry to tell you..." or "I don't mean to complain, but..."

■ **Bury anger in an addiction...**

If you are afraid to express your anger, you may want to push the anger away and sedate yourself with sugary junk foods, alcohol, drugs, or nicotine. See if every time you feel anxiety or anger, you do something to put yourself in a stupor.

You may also try to bury your anger in an obsessive-compulsive addiction, such as gambling, overworking, being a perfectionist, or being obsessed with cleanliness and order. What an addiction can do is take up all of your time so that you ignore your angry feelings. It can also stress your body so you have no energy to confront anyone with your anger. Of course, you end up with no time or energy to do anything else with your life.

■ **Talk yourself out of it...**

When you are afraid to tell someone you feel angry with him, you may try to tell yourself you are not angry or you don't have a good reason to feel angry. You may convince yourself that the person who triggered your anger should not be blamed because he is too young, too old or too crazy.

You could be right that your anger is not appropriate or necessary, or that the person could not withstand being confronted. Just be sure that is the case and that you are not just trying to rationalize your way out of having to confront someone. If so, you need to stick to your feelings.

■ Blame yourself instead...

You may be angry about being mistreated by someone, but afraid he will yell at you if you tell him. You may then convince yourself that you deserve to be mistreated, as a protection from whatever you think are the consequences of confronting him.

Usually, you take the blame for someone's abuse because you have a low opinion of yourself. However, when you do that, you end up feeling even worse about yourself. You also absolve that person of all responsibility for his actions. If you say nothing to him, he may not even know that what he is doing has a negative impact on you. He then has no reason to stop what he is doing.

What happens is:

- **Low self-esteem:** You very much want the love and approval of others.
- **Threat:** You feel threatened by someone's words or behavior.
- **Fear:** You become afraid of losing his love or your freedom.
- **Anger:** You don't think you should be treated this way.
- **Anger-censoring thoughts:** You think he will hurt you if you express your anger.
- **Repressed expression:** You decide to say nothing.
- **Self-blame:** You tell yourself it is your fault he treated you this way.
- **Low self-esteem:** You believe you deserve the mistreatment.

Results of Hiding Anger

When you try to cover up your angry feelings, you create all sorts of problems:

- **You lose touch with your feelings...**

  When you are afraid of expressing your anger, you work hard to push it away when something happens. If you keep doing that, after a while you don't know when you feel angry. You may not realize it until perhaps a day or a week after an event. You may even lose the ability to be in touch with the rest of your emotions.

  When you become freer to express your anger, you stop censoring the feelings. Eventually, you know what you feel at any time, and then you can choose whether or not to express it.

- **You stay angry...**

  When you don't express your anger, it stays with you and you constantly think about how you were wronged by someone and what you did not say to him. Once you decide to let out the anger, it usually ends and you are able to go on with your life.

- **You create aches and pains...**

  Holding in your feelings takes a lot of energy. It is not natural to repress feelings and is actually harder than letting them out. You have to tighten your whole body and this creates tension in your muscles. If you don't release it, you stay charged up but tired at the same time.

  When you are angry with someone, you may unconsciously hold your breath and then feel light-headed. Your anger can make you want to bite him, to say something hurtful, to shout at him, to cry, to punch him. If you try to stop yourself from doing these things, you may develop aches and pains in those parts of your body.

  To prevent yourself from biting, you may clench your jaw during the day and grind your teeth in your sleep. If you wake up most mornings with pain and spasm in your jaw, you may have a condition called TMJ (because it is in the temporal mandibular joint), due to repressed anger.

  To prevent yourself from verbalizing your anger, you may press your lips tightly together until they hurt. You may also tighten your throat muscles until your throat becomes sore.

  You may clench your fist in preparation for hitting someone, but then stiffen your arm to prevent yourself from doing it. If you do this for a period of time, your arm muscles may hurt.

If you think someone is going to verbally or physically attack you for being angry with him, you may tighten your neck and shoulders in anticipation. If you never say you are angry, those muscles may become painful.

When you are angry, you may tighten your stomach muscles. If you hold in your anger, you may end up with indigestion, cramps, or even ulcers.

- **You look for vicarious ways to release your anger...**

When you feel angry and don't express it, you may still need to release it. Participating in the following activities allows you to do that vicariously. You can identify with someone else who is expressing anger or you can express it yourself in a disguised way. See if you do any of these activities and whether it serves as a release of your anger.

- **Own an attack dog.** You may be angry and wish you could attack people. This gives you an opportunity to identify with the dog when see him snap at people.

- **Watch boxing or wrestling matches.** You may wish you could beat up some people you know. This gives you an opportunity to identify with the players in both sports when they punch and attack each other.

- **Demonstrate with groups that fight for causes.** You may be too afraid to stand up by yourself and say you are angry. This gives you an opportunity to express anger while remaining anonymous, and absolves you of most of the responsibility for going against the norm.

- **Take an aggressive position** as a policeman, a prison guard, a nightclub bouncer or a soldier. You may hesitate to show your anger to people you know. This allows you to be hostile with those who break the law or are seen as the enemy, and it gives you a legitimate outlet for your aggression.

- **Go target shooting.** You may wish you could go out and shoot certain people you hate. This allows you to use a gun and pretend you are hitting them.

- **Prefer violent war movies** and detective stories. You may hesitate to act on your aggressive impulses. This allows you to identify with a fictional aggressor who is attacking people and maybe destroying cities, and through him act out the anger you feel.

- **Play video war games.** You may wish you could be aggressive. This lets you pretend to be violent and destroy an enemy, and can give you a release of your anger.

- **Stay with a very angry person.** You may not be able to express the anger that you feel, but you may have someone in your life who expresses his anger by being explosive, by screaming and yelling and by being out of control. Usually, it is upsetting to be with a person who does this. If it bothers you, but you continue to be in a relationship with him, it may be that his loss of control compensates for your being too controlled. Observing him may serve as a release for your anger.

You may choose to do these activities because they give you pleasure, or you may have to do them because you cannot express your anger more directly. Knowing the reason may help you decide if you like the way you handle your angry feelings.

Past Influences

What your parents did when you were a child and they were angry at you or you were angry at them influenced the way you now think about expressing your anger. If it is hard for you to do, you probably picked up negative messages from them.

See how many of the statements in the following chart reflect what your parents did or said when you were a child, and put a check next to them. Then see what effect their behavior had on you.

Check those statements that are true for you:

WHAT MY PARENTS DID	WHAT I THOUGHT
They thought I hated them if I was angry.	☐ I thought anger meant hate.
They punished me for expressing anger.	☐ I thought anger was wrong.
They looked foolish when they got mad.	☐ I thought anger was degrading.
They hurt my feelings if I expressed my anger.	☐ I thought anger was scary.
They showed no anger.	☐ I thought being silent was right.
They got angry but said I couldn't.	☐ I felt confused.
They said express anger, then punished me.	☐ I felt betrayed.
They reacted differently every day.	☐ I did not trust people.
They said anger was rude and uncivilized.	☐ I still think it is.

What did you discover from doing this exercise? Do you see that some of the beliefs you have now about expressing anger come from what your parents did when you were a child? Were they consistent, or were you confused because you never knew what to expect? Did they censor a lot of your expression? Did they practice what they preached? Did they seem threatened by your anger or anger from anyone else?

It serves no purpose to blame your parents for what they did or said. Their behavior and the messages they gave you can provide information to help you understand yourself. Even if their behavior at the time seemed mean, the chances are that it was their way of protecting themselves from anxiety.

When their child is upset or angry about something, many parents think they have to do something to make him feel better. Often they don't know what to do, and so they view the child's feelings as a burden. They would rather not know when their child is upset, and so they do what they can to prevent him from expressing his feelings, especially his anger.

If your parents tried to squelch your anger, it was probably because they found it too threatening. They may have taken your anger at them very personally.

Changing the Messages

No matter what messages you got from your parents about anger, you can discard them if they no longer make sense. If they involve censorship of feelings, you can change them and give yourself permission to be more expressive.

You can help yourself by replacing each irrational belief you have with a more rational one:

Old Message: **If I express anger, I will get hurt.**
New Message: **I can express anger to most people.**

Did you get beaten by a parent for expressing your anger when you were a child? Was it because that person was violent, or was he brought up to be very strict and intolerant of any spontaneity?

No matter what your parents did, they had their own reasons. That doesn't mean that other people will treat you the same way. Most people will accept it if you tell them your feelings. When you want to tell someone you are angry with him, you always have to consider who you are dealing with and then decide what to do. Sometimes, keeping quiet is not productive and confronting someone is worth the risk.

Old Message: **My anger may hurt someone.**
New Message: **I can express anger without being hurtful.**

Do you think that if you let out your anger you would lose control and physically strike someone? Have you actually done that, or do you just think you might? Unless you have a long history of losing control when expressing your anger, there is no reason to think you would ever do that. But even if you were hurtful to others in the past, you can now learn to express it without being hurtful or violent.

You may think that expressing your anger to people who are emotionally fragile will make them fall apart. You need not worry, because most people will defend against what they don't want to hear by tuning it out. You don't have to decide for them what they should or should not be told.

If you say nothing when you are angry, you may avoid physically hurting people. However, they may feel hurt that you did not share your anger with them.

Old Message: **Getting mad at someone means you hate him.**
New Message: **Anger is not hate.**

Did your parents think that when you were angry at them, you were rejecting them? If so, they were probably very insecure. Instead of saying they felt hurt, they may just have told you to keep quiet.

Did your parents yell at you? Did you think it meant they hated you? Anger is not hate; it is a protest about someone's behavior. You can hate what a person is doing and still love him. But if you yell and scream, you can sound as though you hate him.

Screaming and complaining are not constructive ways to show anger, but saying nothing is not better. Families who never fight may seem to have a harmonious relationship, but they actually have limited contact. When you withdraw and remain silent, the other person doesn't know what you want or what you feel. As long as you express your anger in a non-hurtful way, you show you want the relationship to be better.

Old Message: **It is not nice to show anger.**
New Message: **Expressing anger is normal.**

There was a time, especially in the Victorian Era, when it was considered rude for anyone with breeding, especially females, to show anger. Even now, expressing anger, especially in public, is discouraged in England and in some other cultures. Being emotionally expressive, even in public, is the norm mostly in Latin cultures. In most of North America, venting anger in private is considered healthy, but many females feel uncomfortable about doing so.

Do you come from a background that has told you not to express your anger? Do you agree with the messages you got? Do you want to express your anger more openly?

It helps to realize that anger is felt by everyone at some time, and that expressing it is normal. Your anger is just as important as your other emotions, and it is just as valid to say you feel it. No matter what you were taught in the past, you have to now give yourself permission to be angry.

Old Message: **It is useless to express anger.**
New Message: **Anger can create change.**

If you were scolded as a child when you told your parents you were angry, or if they paid no attention to your protests, you may have decided it was better to say nothing. What do you think about it now? Do you think your anger has no impact on anyone? Do you think expressing it is a waste of time?

People may not realize that their behavior is upsetting to you unless you tell them. They may continue to mistreat you if they know you won't complain. If you stand up and fight and demand to be treated well, people have more respect for you, and usually hesitate to bother you again.

If you tell them in a firm, non-attacking manner, there is a chance that they will change. It may be hard to believe that you can have an impact, but if you get in the habit of demanding respect, you will find that you get it.

Getting More in Touch

You still may not be sure what you have been telling yourself that has prevented you from expressing your anger more openly. The following exercise may help.

To do it most effectively, go into a quiet room where you will have no distractions. Choose a comfortable chair to sit in, and sit so you feel no strain.

Read the whole exercise to yourself before you proceed, and when you are ready, take a few deep breaths to feel relaxed. Then close your eyes and follow the instructions. Be aware of your feelings as you do the visualization.

Think about someone who has made you very angry. That person may be in your life now, or may have been at some other time. It doesn't matter whether or not this person is still alive.

Visualize him sitting in a chair near you. Think about why you were angry with him. Try to feel that anger now. Try to remember what you always wanted to say to this person, but never did. This is your chance to let him know how you feel, so go over to him and tell him. Let out all your anger. If you feel like it, hit him, tie him up, or do whatever you feel like doing. See how he reacts to your showing your anger. Hear what he says and see what he does.

When you have said and done all you wish, leave the fantasy and open your eyes.

Examining Your Imagery

What happened when you did this exercise? Answer the following questions to figure out what impact doing it had on you:

■ **Who did you see?**

An imagery exercise is like a dream. You are the creator of all that is in it, the people, the words, and the actions. You see what is significant to you, usually because your feelings about it are unresolved.

Who was in your fantasy? Is this person someone who is in your life now, or someone from your past? Was there more than one person?

Why do you think this particular person appeared, rather than anyone else you know? You probably chose to put this person there, even if he is no longer living, because you are still angry with him.

■ **Did you say all you wanted to?**

If not, why didn't you? Here was an opportunity to call him names, to tell him you were furious with him, and not have him ever know. A lot of people who cannot allow themselves to yell or use strong language also censor their anger in their thoughts. They somehow think they will get in trouble if they even imagine acting tough. Is that true for you?

■ **Did you use any physical force?**

If you didn't, did you want to? What stopped you? Here was an opportunity to get your hostility out without actually hurting anyone. If you thought the person deserved it, you could have imagined taking a rope and tying him to the chair he was sitting in and forcing him to listen to you. You could have hit him on the head, knocked him out of his chair and stepped on him, kicked him, or blindfolded him. You could have drawn a big x and erased him. You could have killed him.

Just because you don't go around hurting people in real life doesn't mean there's anything wrong in imagining it. Doing so will not hurt anyone or make you violent. In fact, when you visualize acting out the anger you feel, you may feel less angry. When you keep anger inside too long, it builds up and may become rage.

■ **Did the person hear all you said?**

How did the person in your fantasy respond to you when you said you were angry? Did he say anything, or did he sit passively in his chair? Did he tune you out? Did you make him listen by repeating yourself and being insistent, or did you give up?

■ **How did you feel during the fantasy?**

Did you allow yourself to feel your anger, or did you censor it and feel nothing? Did you yell and then feel relieved?

How do you feel now? Do you still feel angry? Do you feel a sense of relief because you got the anger out? If not, you might want to do the exercise again and this time give yourself permission to really feel your feelings and express them.

■ **What have you done in reality with this person?**

Have you ever talked to him as you did in the fantasy? If so, how has he reacted? If you have never said anything, why haven't you? What do you think he would do if you did? How do you know how he would react?

If this person is in your life now and you still have things to tell him, perhaps you want to take a chance and do it. If he tunes you out, you have to insist he hear you. If he gets nasty, you have to tell him you won't put up with it.

Answers From Others

This exercise was given to all of the people who were members of various anger management groups. It might be helpful to see what two of them saw in their fantasies and what it meant to them:

Dolly was a 45 year old married woman with a family. She was always very polite and brought up to repress all of her angry feelings.

In her fantasy, she saw a cousin who always put her down. She felt very angry with her and hit her with a stick. She saw her cousin break into pieces. Then Dolly hit her cousin again and she disappeared.

After telling her story, Dolly talked about how she was always angry in real life with her cousin, but would never dare say anything to her. In fact, she felt guilty about having done it in the fantasy, and especially about having hit her.

As she got more in touch with her anger, Dolly talked about how she had been criticized by her mother many times in the past. She believed her mother would fall apart if she knew Dolly was angry, so she never said anything to her. She always felt guilty because she thought being angry with your mother was wrong.

Dolly had not allowed herself to visualize her mother in the fantasy, but felt safe making her cousin a symbol of her mother. When she expressed her anger in the imagery exercise by hitting her, something she considered very extreme, she saw her cousin literally "fall apart". She began to cry when she saw that destroying her cousin in the fantasy was like destroying her mother in real life.

At the same time, Dolly felt some of her anger slip away. She felt sad about the many years she had wasted being full of guilt and self-doubts, blaming herself for her mother's verbal attacks on her. This exercise paved the way for her to make some positive changes.

Laura was a young, single woman living by herself. She also had a hard time expressing her anger to anyone, mostly because she never believed anyone would listen to her.

In her fantasy, she saw her parents sitting together on a couch. She went over to tell them that she was angry with them for never paying attention to her. Before she could say anything, they told her not to bother them. She then gave up and left the room.

Laura always had considered her parents to be smarter and more powerful than her. She thought that if she stood up to her parents, they would win and she would lose. Even in her fantasy, she censored her behavior and had as little impact as she did in her life.

Laura was urged to do the exercise again at home and to imagine herself powerful and assertive in it. She did, and this time, she told off her parents in the fantasy. Seeing herself as stronger, even in a dream-like exercise, gave Laura much more of a chance to become that way.

An Additional Exercise

When anger is expressed, the energy it took to hold it in is released. Often, this makes the anger disappear. The anger you feel when someone mistreats you is never as great as it becomes when you say nothing and think about it later. When you wait to express your anger, it can grow bigger with time.

If you are angry with someone who is no longer around, you obviously have no way to confront him. The problem is that your anger may still be there, so you have to find a way to get past it.

What might help is writing a letter to this person, which, of course, you will not mail. When you write it, let out all of the feelings you have stored up. Don't be polite and don't censor anything. No one is going to see it but you.

When you have said all you want to say, read the letter if you want to, and then throw it out. Be aware of how you feel both during the exercise and after you have finished.

6. BECOMING MORE DIRECT

Passive-Aggressive Expression of Anger

You may want to express your anger and get back at people who hurt you, but you may be afraid to express it openly and have them know you are doing it. That means when you are angry with someone, you express your anger at him indirectly by being passive-aggressive. You either manipulate him or you put the anger somewhere else. What you may do is:

■ **Say you are angry about something else...**

A young woman was very insecure and was always thinking her husband didn't love her. She was constantly angry with him. When she went into the bathroom and saw that he had left the cap off the toothpaste, she thought that it showed that he had no interest in her needs. She didn't want him to know she felt hurt, so she told him she was angry that he had not put the cap back on.

Instead of saying she was angry about being rejected, this woman talked about the toothpaste cap. There was no way her husband could figure out why she so upset, or what the cap really symbolized for her.

When you tell someone what you are angry about, it often reveals your fears and anxieties. You may not like doing that and choose instead to say you are angry about something trivial. Sometimes, you may not even realize that what you say you are angry about is not the real issue.

■ **Show anger to someone safer...**

When you are afraid to confront someone with your anger, you may instead pick on someone you think is less likely to hurt you.

You may be afraid to tell your boss you are angry with him, but still feel the anger when you go home. You may then transfer your anger onto someone in your family and yell at him for the slightest thing, knowing that he will still love you.

You may be angry with your spouse, but instead of yelling at him, you may feel safer yelling at your child. If doing this gets your spouse upset, you may use it to indirectly get back at him.

You may have pent-up anger at someone because you are afraid to express it, and transfer it onto the people with whom you play a sport or conduct business. You may play the sport in a fierce manner, just so you can see them lose the game, or be ruthless in business so you can see them lose their money.

The trouble with doing all this is that you are not directly confronting the person you are angry with, so he has no idea what you want. Also, the person you yell at or try to defeat feels hurt and doesn't know that your anger is not really at him.

- **Show anger to someone similar...**

Recently, a serial killer raped and killed over a dozen women, all in their twenties, with heart-shaped faces and long, dark hair parted in the middle. He told police that his first victim was a woman who had rejected him. His anger at her was repeated in his killing of the other women.

It is likely that the first woman he killed was not the real trigger for his anger. Some other female, perhaps a mother or a sister, may have hurt and rejected him in his childhood. That hurt turned to rage, and the women he killed may have resembled her, so he was killing her again and again.

Obviously, this is an unusual case, but many people do get angry at someone who has similar personality traits or appearance to someone else. If you were angry with someone and never told him, his face and his being may still be with you, even if he is no longer around. Every time you meet someone who is similar to him, you may unfairly project your anger onto him.

- **Generalize the anger....**

It is sometimes easier to be angry at an impersonal group than it is to confront an individual. Recently, a serial killer came into a university in Florida and randomly shot at many female students. He screamed that he hated feminists. He didn't know these women, but they represented the type of women toward whom he had rage. He generalized his anger toward one or two feminists to any group of women he believed were also feminists.

In the same way, a female who is abused by her father or brother may become a militant feminist who hates all men; a male who is mistreated by his mother may become a male chauvinist who hates women; a person who is abused by both parents may become a loner who distrusts everyone.

You may be angry and prejudiced toward a particular group of people for their ethnic background, their race, their religion, or even their gender. Perhaps you make statements that stereotype them, or you make jokes about them. Perhaps you refuse to associate with them. If so, you have to wonder whether the anger you feel toward someone who hurt you in the past has been transferred onto a group of people who are similar in some way.

■ **Use anger to hide other feelings...**

Todd found out that the company he worked for the past twelve years was cutting back to save money and he might be laid off. He was scared that he wouldn't be able to pay his bills or find another job. To hide his fear from his family, and because they were a constant reminder of his responsibilities, he became irritable and angry with them.

It is not unusual to use anger to hide fear, or to blame someone for causing you anxiety. A woman may lose sight of her child in a shopping mall and feel terrified, but when he is found, she may yell at him. Her anger provides her with a release of her anxiety, but she also may blame him for being lost and causing her to worry.

■ **Use humor to hide anger...**

You may try to disguise your anger by telling jokes that poke fun at some group or individual; by telling wife-bashing stories to others in front of your wife; or by interrupting others when they speak in order to make puns. You may tease someone about his appearance, his name, his job, his habits, or an impediment.

In every case, you appear witty without anyone else realizing that behind your humor is hostility. You get laughs at someone else's expense and you make him feel foolish and uncomfortable. Doing these things allows you to put others on the defensive and put yourself in the spotlight.

■ **Be promiscuous...**

Having an affair with one person while married to someone else is not usually about falling for that person. Being promiscuous is about using a lover instead of words to let your partner know you are angry. Maybe you want more attention or affection. Maybe your partner is abusing you and you think doing something shocking will end the abuse.

Even if you keep your affair a secret and your partner doesn't find out about it, having the affair is passive-aggressive if it is about getting revenge. If your partner does find out about the affair, it may be because you unconsciously want that to happen.

It is unfortunate if your relationship breaks up as a result because then neither of you gets to work on the angry feelings that may have triggered it in the first place.

■ **Be indecisive...**

A woman dated a man who never said what he wanted or what he was thinking. He had her pick a movie or a restaurant for them to go to, and went even when he didn't like her choice. If the movie was a dud or the restaurant was crowded or the food was only fair, he blamed her and was disagreeable.

Because this man never made a decision, he never had to take responsibility for the outcome and could blame the other person. He appeared to be ineffective and complaisant, but he was expressing anger by being indecisive and then manipulating others.

A man was indecisive about whether or not he wanted to divorce his wife. He began an affair with another woman, but when his wife found out, he told her he would end it. He still wanted his wife to be there for him. He did not end the affair, but his wife believed he would and she stayed. At the same time, he did not leave his wife as he told the other woman he would.

This man could not make a decision because he didn't want to be blamed for hurting either woman. He also was angry with his wife and enjoyed putting her in a position of no power with his indecisiveness.

■ **Eat compulsively...**

When you over or undereat because it upsets someone, you use food and weight to passive-aggressively act out your anger.

Marcie wanted to lose weight, but found it hard to give up being fat. It was the only way she knew to get back at her husband for not paying attention to her. Instead of telling him directly that she was angry, she overate and gained weight. This upset her husband and he kept nagging her to lose weight. This angered her even more and led to more food binges.

Marcie began her acting out behavior in childhood. She was angry with her mother for not being very supportive, but she was afraid to tell her. She discovered that her mother would be really upset if Marcie did not look perfect and that being overweight could be a way to really hurt her mother. At the same time, her mother would not know that Marcie was staying fat to retaliate, so she could get away with being angry at her.

Marcie was using her body to express her anger. Even though her mother was no longer in her life or even alive, she still went on food binges to anger her. She also did it to hurt her husband because he treated her as her mother had.

When Marcie was finally able to tell her husband what she wanted, she no longer had to overeat. Then, she could have the body that she wanted, not the one she used for communicating her anger.

Some people use starving and being underweight in the same way as Marcie had used being overweight. That does not mean that it is always passive-aggressive to eat compulsively. The true test is whether the behavior is upsetting to someone else, and whether that is why it is being done.

■ **Use money to control...**

You may do something with money that gives you control over another person as a way to get back at him.

Al complained about how his sister, who lived alone and had a modest income, never seemed to have any money. She frequently called him on the phone and told him it was his duty as a brother to help her out.

Al felt sorry for his sister and was uncomfortable about having much more money than she had, so he gave her money any time she asked him for it. The problem was that she always seemed to spend it impulsively and then plead poverty again.

Al finally realized that his sister was very jealous of him for having a fancy house and other luxuries, and spending his money was her revenge. Seeing that he was being manipulated made it easier for Al to turn down his sister's requests after that.

A woman was a compulsive shopper. She frequently went to a mall and bought expensive jewelry and clothes, charging them on the credit card account she shared with her husband. She didn't need what she bought, but she could not stop herself. When her husband saw the bills, he was furious. The woman always apologized, but then she did it again.

The woman felt neglected by her husband. He was an executive for a large company and spent a lot of time at meetings and conferences. She had a lot of free time and resented his being out. Instead of saying anything directly to him, she spent their money to get his attention and to upset him.

Actually, the man was spending more time away than was necessary because he could not stand his wife's moodiness. When she learned to verbalize her feelings, he was more willing to be home. In time, she had her needs met and stopped the compulsive shopping.

A woman brought her 14 year old daughter to counseling because she had caught her daughter taking money from her wallet. She tried punishing her for stealing and for being insolent when she scolded her, but her daughter seemed to act worse.

The girl complained that her mother was too controlling, had too many rules, and treated her unfairly. She said that any time she had expressed her anger about it, her mother punished her.

The girl had found a way to get back at her mother and get away with it. If nothing changed, the girl might find more serious ways to act out her anger.

Naturally, if the girl did commit a crime, she would have to pay the consequences. However, it was important to rectify the situation that created her need to indirectly express her anger. That meant the woman had to be firm about her needs, but still let her daughter express herself more freely and do more of what she wanted. In time, the girl might no longer need to steal or be a behavior problem.

Sue had a part-time job, but whatever she earned, she used to buy groceries. When she needed money for anything else, she had to ask her husband for it. Sometimes, he refused to give it to her. Asking him for money made Sue feel like a child getting an allowance.

Sue's husband liked putting her in a position where he could have all the power. It was the way he expressed his anger toward her, never verbalizing it. In fact, he never discussed anything with Sue.

When Sue first came to counseling, she was very passive. She accepted the financial arrangement as it was, even though she felt trapped by it. She thought that her husband would get mad and give her nothing if she spoke up, and that it was not really proper for a wife to do that anyway.

After many sessions, Sue realized she had rights within the relationship and did not have to allow her husband to manipulate her. She saw that in order for her to function as an adult, she had to do something about the money issue. She became assertive and insisted that the bank account be in both of their names. When Sue no longer had to go to her husband for money, she could concentrate on whether she even wanted to live with him.

■ **Manipulate with time...**

• **Be late:**

Every time Sherry was supposed to meet Vicky for lunch in a restaurant, she would show up late. She always had an excuse that sounded legitimate to Vicky, like being held up in heavy traffic, getting a last minute phone call, or having to look for her car keys. Vicky believed the excuses the first few times Sherry was late, but after that, she wondered if they were true or if Sherry's lateness was intentional.

Being late and making Vicky wait for her put Sherry in a power position. Vicky would think she was being stood up and feel rejected until Sherry arrived; she would be inconvenienced; and if her time was limited, she would have to rush.

Vicky needed to tell Sherry what her being late was doing to the relationship and see if Sherry was at all concerned. If it seemed that she was not, it would be better for Vicky if she stopped making appointments with Sherry.

- **Take too long:**

Maybe you make others late when they have to go somewhere with you. Maybe you take forever to get dressed, or wait until the last minute to get ready, or can never find your wallet or your keys when it is time to leave.

If you can't help it because you are a poor time manager, your behavior cannot be considered a manipulation. You just may not have a sense of time that allows you to estimate how long it takes to get ready. Someone might have to tell you the appointment is an hour before it really is so you will be ready on time, or keep reminding you of the time while you are getting ready, but this will probably annoy you.

You need to consider whether your behavior is about anger and getting even. If so, trying to verbalize your anger might serve to end your chronic lateness.

- **Be early:**

A woman dated a man who always came to pick her up earlier than the time they had agreed upon. He claimed to have forgotten the correct time. Since she did not expect him then, she was usually not ready and he had to wait for her. She felt rushed and very uncomfortable with his being there.

Showing up early could have been the result of a misunderstanding or a bad memory if it happened a couple of times, but if this man did it repeatedly, he probably had underlying hostility. His actions clearly put the woman at a disadvantage, and he knew it. If she continued to see him without discussing this issue, the relationship would probably be doomed.

Making someone wait by showing up late, surprising someone by coming early, or making someone late by taking your time to get ready are all ways to express anger indirectly. They can give you a sense of control over others for making them uncomfortable.

- ■ **Use guilt or pity...**

Dana and her mother lived in different towns. Whenever Dana called her mother, she was scolded for not calling more often. Her mother would say she felt rejected and that it was Dana's fault. Dana would then feel guilty and call again, but her mother would still scold her.

Instead of her mother saying she wanted a closer relationship with Dana, she put Dana on the defensive, tried to get her pity, and tried to make her feel guilty. This made Dana call more often, but it did not make them closer.

If someone tells you he is angry with you and you remind him how much you have done for him, you are manipulating him to shift the focus away from his anger. You may succeed in making him feel guilty, but he will also be angry about not being heard.

■ **Act helpless....**

When a woman asked her husband to empty the dishwasher, he claimed ignorance about where to put the dishes. When he needed a screwdriver or some other tool, he said he couldn't find it and asked her to get it. He waited for her to fix anything that broke, to figure out the directions on a map when they went anywhere, or to operate a simple appliance when he wanted to use it.

This man was quite capable of doing these things himself, but he was angry with his wife for not giving him enough attention. He acted helpless in order to get her to wait on him. Maybe you manipulate others this way instead of saying what you really want.

■ **Use illness...**

Carla, 20, was always saying she was sick. When she did, her parents and her brother fussed over her. They took her to many doctors, but none of them found anything wrong, and several suggested that the problem was psychological.

Carla was angry with her family for neglecting her in the past and had now found a way to get them upset. She got pleasure from seeing her family concerned about her. She enjoyed the attention she got from them and from the doctors. Until she learned to express her anger openly and to ask for attention when she wanted it, she could not stop using illness to manipulate.

■ **Create worry...**

You may indirectly express your anger by doing dangerous things, such as mountain climbing, sky diving, or driving very fast, in order to worry someone. You may use drugs, or eat junk foods for the same reason.

A girl of fifteen stopped doing her schoolwork. When her teachers told her parents that she was failing most of her subjects, they were upset and embarrassed.

The girl was angry with her parents for nagging her about her grades. She also believed that they only loved her when she did well. Her poor school performance was a way to get back at them, and to find out if they would still be there for her. Not only was she acting out her anger, but she was also spoiling her chances to go to college.

■ Be rebellious...

Brian, 16, lived at home. His parents were upset with his long, unruly hair and his sloppy clothes. The more they complained, the less care he took.

Brian was angry with his parents for being critical, and he used his appearance to get back at them.

Dan, 25, felt stifled growing up. His parents had always been very rigid in their views. He tried to shock them with extreme actions, such as smoking pot, wearing outlandish clothes, and having wild friends. He also dated a woman of another religion, which very much upset his parents.

Dan knew just what would bother his parents the most, so he did those things in their presence. He wanted to tell them without words that he was angry with their imposing their stodginess on him.

Characteristics of Passive-Aggressive Behavior

What each of these behaviors has in common is that:

■ It is done to show another person...

If you do something just for you, your actions are not truly passive-aggressive. Being passive-aggressive implies doing something to someone. Even if that person is no longer living, he can be the reason you choose the behavior.

It is not passive-aggressive to overeat or take drugs, for instance, if you do it just for yourself. It can become passive-aggressive if you do it because you know someone you are angry with will find out.

It is not passive-aggressive to lock yourself out of your car. It can become passive-aggressive if you do it frequently in order to have a friend come and drive you back home.

■ **It affects someone negatively...**

If no one else is affected by what you do, the behavior cannot be considered passive-aggressive. It must be done because you know someone you are angry with hates your doing it and will be upset about it. If you know he is not, you probably will find some other behavior to act out your anger at him.

Why You Are Passive-Aggressive

There are many reasons why you may choose to express anger in a passive-aggressive way:

■ **To appear innocent...**

Being passive-aggressive allows you to hide your anger behind socially acceptable behavior that makes the manipulation difficult to identify. Others see what you are doing, but they cannot say with certainty that it is meant to hurt them. Therefore, you can annoy and manipulate people without their realizing why you are doing it, and you don't get blamed for your actions.

■ **To avoid confrontation...**

If you openly tell people you are angry, they may not like it and you may have to face their anger, their retaliation, or their rejection. If you do it in a passive-aggressive way, your anger is so subtle that they are not likely to notice it.

■ **To feel powerful...**

If you are not usually able to stand your ground when people hurt you, it is difficult to have a sense of your own power. By being passive-aggressive, you can manipulate others and get them to behave the way you want. This can give you an illusion of power.

You may not always realize that what you are doing is passive-aggressive. You may not be aware that you are very angry with someone and that you are doing something in order to manipulate him. That means you can fool both the other person and yourself into looking at your behavior as accidental, and not as purposefully hostile. You may be able to fool your conscious mind, but it is your unconscious that often determines your behavior.

Disadvantages

Being passive-aggressive is not a good idea because:

- **You hurt yourself...**

Almost all passive-aggressive behavior is self-destructive. Over-eating, undereating, eating junk foods, and using drugs or alcohol are all harmful to your body. Losing things, performing poorly at a job or in school, spending money compulsively, being in constant debt, shop-lifting, gambling, and acting helpless are all harmful to your life.

When you express your anger in ways that are more direct, you do not get hurt. You may initially decide to do something as a way to bug someone, but when you realize it is hurting you more, you may decide to stop doing it.

- **You hurt others...**

When you use sarcasm, teasing, promiscuity, guilt, lateness, or any other behavior to manipulate people, they become annoyed or feel hurt, and they resent you. If you express your anger openly in an assertive way, you hurt no one.

- **It is difficult to do...**

It is really hard work to be indirect. You have to think up behaviors that will be annoying, spend a lot of time figuring out how to manipulate someone so that it won't be detected, hold in your anger, and maybe lie to hide what you really feel. It takes much less effort to be open about your anger.

Testing Yourself

The chart below lists many behaviors that involve expressing anger in an indirect way. Check off the ones that you think you may do in order to get back at someone. Keep in mind that you may be doing some of them without knowing the reason.

Check those items that are true for you:

■ MANIPULATE by having annoying behavior

☐ use sarcasm ☐ be a no-show ☐ spend compulsively

☐ use targeted humor ☐ arrive unannounced ☐ be in debt

☐ tease ☐ be late ☐ fail to return loans

☐ be promiscuous ☐ delay others ☐ dress sloppily

☐ use guilt ☐ use pity ☐ use drugs, alcohol

☐ overeat ☐ act helpless ☐ blame others

☐ undereat ☐ lose things ☐ shoplift

☐ eat junk ☐ perform poorly ☐ other

■ USE DIVERSION

☐ feel scared and show anger instead

☐ feel angry about major issue, say it is about trivial one

☐ feel angry with someone, pick on another instead who is safer

---

Do you do a lot of the things on the list? What do most of them seem to be about? Are they about appearance, about using your body, or about time? What can you learn about yourself from your answers? Do you seem to avoid putting your anger where it belongs?

Making Changes

When something triggers your anger, you can help yourself to express your anger more directly by answering the following questions:

■ **Who am I angry with?**

When you feel angry, try to pinpoint exactly who is the object of your anger. Otherwise, you may yell at someone else who happens to be there.

■ **Have I told that person?**

Have you expressed your anger to that person? If not, why haven't you? Are you afraid that he will retaliate and you won't be able to defend yourself? Have you been yelling at someone else instead? Why have you chosen that person? Does it seem safer to tell him? Is he a symbol of someone else? It is not fair to other people to use them that way. It is also not productive.

■ **How have I expressed my anger?**

Have you expressed it with words or with actions, such as overeating, teasing or doing anything else to manipulate or annoy someone? Words, as long as they are not hurtful, are the only appropriate vehicle for expressing anger, and the only one that clearly communicates what you feel.

■ **Is my passive-aggressive behavior effective?**

Does the person you are trying to send a message to know what you want? Has he stopped mistreating you, or is your behavior making him treat you worse? Is your behavior harmful to you? Maybe it is time to find a better way to express your anger.

7. ENDING YOUR AGGRESSION

Characteristics of Being Aggressive

You may express your anger differently at different times, and with different people, but there is one way that is probably more frequent. If you are not usually passive or passive-aggressive and don't try to hide what you feel, you may express anger by being aggressive. That means that you behave as follows:

■ **You are arrogant...**

You act as though you feel superior to others and look down on them. You are bossy and controlling at work and at home with your family, and you tell them what to do. You think you know what is good for them and you try to make decisions for them. You are furious if people don't listen. You blame them for everything, and you never admit to making mistakes. You insist on getting your own way and you make a lot of demands, even if they are unreasonable. You are hard to please and you are never satisfied when people do things for you. In a restaurant, you may constantly order the waiter around. At a party, a business meeting, or a family gathering, you usually monopolize the conversation. People probably resent you and feel intimidated.

■ **You are invasive...**

You do not respect people's boundaries. Instead, you invade their personal space, even when you don't know them, by asking personal questions, opening their mail, and dropping in to see them without first calling. You physically invade the space of other people by touching them when you talk to them. You stand very close, slap them on the back, poke them in the ribs, or tap them on the shoulder. This may be the way you try to get someone's attention, make sure he doesn't leave, see if he is still there, or let him know you are in charge.

If you observe animals, you will notice that most of them will not allow anyone to get too close to them. Those in the wild are very protective of their territory, as well as of their bodies and their young. Even your own pet will probably not let others pet him if he doesn't know them. Many people feel the same way about being touched without permission.

■ **You attack verbally...**

You speak sharply in a loud voice, and your voice escalates as you talk, until you are shouting and yelling. You may do it even when you are not angry.

You use hurtful words to criticize others, to find fault with everything they do and to call them insulting names. Your sentences begin with *you are*.... Those attacked usually feel insulted or hurt, so you often regret what you said.

Your words are violent. You talk about wanting to bash, attack, and destroy bad drivers on the road, politicians you disagree with, inefficient clerks, clumsy family members, and anonymous they who cause you to pay tolls, wait in traffic, hit potholes, or pay high taxes.

Using curse words makes your language violent. They are graphic, describing bodily functions about the toilet or sex. You may use them when you are not angry, but when you curse in anger, the words mean hate and destruction. Anyone you say them to will feel offended.

■ **Your actions are violent...**

You can become so angry that you have difficulty restraining your impulses. When you don't get your way, you may throw things, push, slap or punch people, and even try to kill them. That means your anger has become rage, and your aggression is in the form of violence.

Rating Your Aggression

Are you aggressive? Fill in the following chart to find out.

Check those statements that are true for you:

- ☐ I ask personal questions of everyone.
- ☐ I touch others when I speak.
- ☐ I drop in uninvited on people.
- ☐ I want everything done my way.
- ☐ I tell others what to do.
- ☐ I interrupt others when they speak.
- ☐ I talk in a loud voice.
- ☐ I call others names when I am angry.
- ☐ I criticize others more than I praise them.
- ☐ I frequently use curse words.
- ☐ I sometimes hit people.
- ☐ I hurt those I love.
- ☐ People often say I hurt them.
- ☐ I lose control when I am angry.
- ☐ I say things I later regret.

Did you check more than half of the statements as being true? If you did, you can say you are aggressive. What do the people who know you say about you? Do they think you hate them when you don't? Do you ever correct that impression? Is your language too violent? If that is not how you really want to express your anger, you should think about changing it. If you only feel powerful when you yell or use curse words, you may need to work on improving your self-esteem.

Results of Being Aggressive

Any time you are aggressive, you have a negative impact on others. You say things you later regret, you send out a message of disdain and disrespect, and you hurt people. You may feel powerful when you see that people cringe in your presence and are too intimidated to stand up to you. You may like talking louder than others and forcing them to give you attention when you talk. You may even delude yourself into thinking people like your manner. It is doubtful, however, that anyone could, since behind aggression is hostility and an arrogance about feeling superior. What happens is that:

• Some people may feel inadequate in your presence and dislike you for it.

• Some people may resent you and want to avoid you.

• Some people may tune you out when you speak.

• Some people may do what you want out of fear, but not respect.

• Some people may feel attacked, get angry and want revenge.

• Some people may retaliate and fire you, hit you, or throw you out.

As you can see, being aggressive is not likely to make you popular. It is likely to cause you embarrassment and get you into trouble in your relationships.

Looking at Your Beliefs

Why would you do something that is really so unappealing and hurtful to others? Why be a bully? If you are aggressive, you are probably basing your actions on your beliefs. Look at the chart below and see what you usually think.

> **Check those statements that are true for you:**
> **BELIEFS**
>
> ☐ I have to speak loudly or I will be ignored.
> ☐ I must fight for my place or others will get what I want.
> ☐ I must show that I am in charge or I will be pushed around.
> ☐ I must be intimidating or I will be hurt.
> ☐ I must make demands or I will get nothing.

If you checked most of these statements, you apparently believe that people are not interested in what you have to say or who you are, and that you have to constantly be on the offense with them. Your aggression is your protection from being hurt or being controlled by others.

When you hold these beliefs, it is usually because of things that happened to you in your past, especially when you were a child. Look at the chart below to understand how your beliefs might have come from what you experienced in your childhood

> **Check those statements that are true for you:**
> **CHILDHOOD EXPERIENCE**
>
> ☐ I only got what I wanted when I had temper tantrums.
> ☐ I had to compete with my siblings to get any attention.
> ☐ I was intimidated by __my mother __my father.
> ☐ I was __verbally __physically abused by __my mother __my father.
> ☐ I was ignored by my parents.

Usually, there is a correlation between your behavior, your beliefs, and your past experiences. Are you aggressive because you did not get the attention you wanted as a child? Were you ignored? Were you abused? Did you come from a very aggressive family? Did your siblings get more attention than you?

As a result, do you think the only way to make it in this world is by fighting for your place? Do you think you have to push people around to show them that you are in charge? Do you think people will hurt you unless they feel intimidated? Do you think that you have to be over-bearing to prevent that from happening?

If you are aggressive now when you interact with other people, it is likely that you felt abused as a child and thought that the only way to survive on your own was by acting tough and intimidating people. If you were ignored, it might have made you think you have to be very demanding or scream and yell to get what you want.

Becoming Less Aggressive

Are you satisfied with being an aggressive person? Would you prefer to have a gentler attitude about people and be able to express your anger in a less destructive way? You can if you make an effort to do the following:

■ **Change your attitude...**

Being aggressive is usually a facade to hide your insecurities. You want the love and approval you did not get in childhood. If you think that being arrogant and intimidating people is the way to get it, you may be surprised to find that it actually has the opposite effect. If you are hostile and abusive, you can expect people to feel angry or hurt. You cannot think your actions have no impact on others. You cannot expect them to pretend you did nothing, that it never happened. They probably resent you and may want to hurt you. They do what they can to avoid you. Instead of getting their love, you get the same mistreatment you got in childhood.

If you can't deal with their rejection, you really have to change your attitude about relating to people and treat them no worse than you want to be treated. You need to do the following:

• **Don't push yourself in anywhere unannounced.** When you call people on the phone, ask them if they have time to talk to you. If someone is in a room with the door closed, knock before entering and only after they invite you in. Respect the people in your life and allow them their privacy. Your needs cannot always take precedence over those of others.

- **Stop interrupting other people when they are talking,** and learn to be a better listener. Force yourself to keep quiet until someone has finished talking. When people find it hard to complete a sentence without your butting in, they may stop talking to you, or they may become hostile or ignore you when you speak. When you are less invasive, people are more interested in what you have to say.

- **Stop being controlling.** When someone's behavior doesn't change your life in any way, it is not really your business. When someone does something different from the way you would do it, try to keep quiet about it. It is not your place to tell other people what to do unless their actions hurt you. It makes no difference if it is a stranger or a close friend or family member.

  You can avoid hassles with your children about how they dress, how they wear their hair, who their friends are, how they spend their money, and how clean they keep their rooms if you remember this. It is only right to interfere if what they are doing is harmful to you or to themselves. It is only right to give an opinion if you are asked for it, but if you aren't, don't say anything.

- **Admit that you are not perfect,** that you are scared or confused. Then people see you as more human and can feel connected to your vulnerability. They also have more respect for you than when you act arrogant.

- **Stop blaming others for what they do.** Try to give them a chance to explain what their motives are before you jump to conclusions. Don't assume that everyone wants to hurt you, because then you walk around with a chip on your shoulder and try to attack people before they can attack you. When you wait to get the facts, you may find out that most of the time people are not motivated by anything that has to do with you.

- **Take responsibility for your anger.** Don't blame others for making you lose your temper or for being hostile. You are choosing how to express your anger. Even when people do things that make you angry, they don't make you scream and yell.

- ■ **Change the way you express your anger...**
  If you only got what you wanted as a child after you had a temper

tantrum, you learned to express anger by yelling and throwing a fit. You didn't learn to use words instead. What do you do now?

- **Talk more softly.** When you are loud, people may appear to listen to you. The chances are, though, that they feel intimidated and are just going through the motions. They may be paying more attention to their fear than to your words. In fact, some people will tune you out when you yell. If you usually talk as though everyone is deaf, you have to make a conscious effort to speak more quietly. Try speaking in a whisper and see if people pay attention.

- **Stop using swear words.** Otherwise, people pick up your hostility and feel angry. They don't make the changes you want, and in fact, may become resistant to change just to spite you.

- **Express your anger without attacking**, without name-calling. When people feel hurt, they are not likely to want to treat you well.

- **Let others defend themselves.** If you are abusive to someone close to you and insult him, curse at him, blame him for something, be sure you don't leave the room before he has a chance to defend himself. Doing that is cruel because it just leaves him feeling hurt. It also deprives you of resolving the issue that triggered your anger in the first place.
  The person getting the last word is not necessarily the winner. Staying in the room could lead to communication between both of you and perhaps lead to constructive change.

- **Stop being physically abusive.** Besides being against the law, violence is cruel and unfair. No matter how angry you feel, you have no right to hurt anyone. If you are out of control and cannot stop yourself, you need to seek help from community centers, counselors, or hotlines that deal with abuse. Look in the phone book or the local newspaper, ask your religious leader or your friends for the name of a therapist. If you don't stop the violent outbursts, you may kill someone and end up in prison.
  Even if your aggression is not in the form of violence, it may be hurting your relationships or taking a toll on your health. If it is, you might want to seek a professional counselor to learn how to manage your anger. It would also be beneficial to learn meditation and

relaxation exercises, and to engage in some physical activity.

- **Express your anger when you feel it.** Strange as it may seem, a lot of your aggression can come from keeping too much of your anger in. People do things that annoy you, you say nothing to them at the time, you harbor the anger until it builds and becomes much stronger, and then you act aggressive and hostile to everyone. The more you don't tell someone you are angry with him, the more likely you are to take that anger out on others. When you get the anger out at the time something happens, it usually disappears.

It is not easy to stop being aggressive. You may not realize the effect you have on others, or if you do, how to change it. Mostly, being aggressive is about feeling hurt, so you may need help to deal with that before you can give up the aggression.

Part Three

COPING WITH ANGRY PEOPLE

This section is about what to do when you meet people who hide their angry feelings, try to manipulate you, or are abusive to you. It shows you how to change some of your ideas so that you don't take it personally when people are angry with you.

8. SEEING HIDDEN ANGER IN OTHERS

Why People Are Angry

Wherever you go, you run into angry people. They may or may not be angry with you, and even when it seems as though they are, their anger may be about other things. They may express it to you just because you are there. You can't take it personally when people are angry because:

- **They may be worried or frustrated about something...**

You never know when you get scolded by someone if he is really angry with you or if he has something on his mind that is upsetting him and he is set off by something you say. Venting their anger at you may relieve tension for many of the people you encounter in a day. They may feel frustrated about being prevented from doing something, or they may be worried and anxious.

Walter, 40, owned a small bookstore, and business was beginning to fail. He had trouble paying some of his bills, and was concerned about supporting his wife and children. The more worried he was, the more irritable he became. On some level, he resented their existence. Seeing them reminded him of his financial problems, and he yelled at them for any little thing they did.

- **They may be really angry with someone else...**

Amy, 35, had been busy all day with her baby, who wasn't feeling well, and it made her fall behind schedule. When her husband Jim came home and saw dinner was not ready, he got furious. Amy didn't get a chance to tell him what happened, and he didn't tell her what he was so angry about it. He had received a poor review from his boss that day, and that it made him overly sensitive. He took Amy's lateness with dinner to mean she didn't care about him any more than his boss did.

A person can act angry with you but really be angry with someone he talked to just before seeing you. He can be carrying around anger about someone in his past, and your appearance, your personality, your actions, or something you say can remind him of it. Since you are there and the other person isn't, you can become the target of his anger.

■ **They may be angry that they need you..**

Wayne, 23, lived with his parents because he had not found a full-time job since graduating from college. He was angry that he could not afford to move out. He wanted to be on his own, but at this point, he needed his parents to help him.

Although he appreciated their help, he acted disagreeable when they did. This was because he had some fears about being on his own, and when his parents treated him well, it made it even harder for him to think about leaving. Without realizing it, he was trying to create more distance between them to make the separation easier.

Sheila, 18, was leaving for college, and the closer the time got, the more she fought with her mother. She was the last of three daughters to leave home, and she was aware that her mother worried about no longer being needed. Sheila also had some fears about living on campus. Arguing relieved some of her guilt and anxiety by making her mother glad to get rid of her and by making Sheila feel less attached to her mother.

If you are in a similar situation with someone, try to see what his anger is about. If you are taking care of a child or an elderly parent and he acts hostile, it may be because he doesn't like being helpless.

■ **They may be afraid of intimacy...**

Some people won't let you get too close because they don't want to risk rejection at a later time. They use anger to protect themselves. They pick a fight with you so you will stay away from them. Then, they can be sure you won't be close enough to reject them. They prefer the loneliness they then experience to the anxiety that closeness brings.

■ **They may not like your seeing their faults...**

There are people who are convinced you will reject them if you see that they are less than perfect. They anticipate being hurt for it. If you are present when people like that do something wrong, they get angry with you and attack you before you can say anything.

In all of these situations, angry people are really making statements about themselves, not you. They are revealing their frustrations, their insecurities, their hurt feelings, or their inability to put the anger where it belongs. They are not really angry with you. You are there, but they could just as easily show anger to someone else who was on the scene.

Triggering Less Anger in Others

Sometimes, people are angry with you because of something you did to antagonize them. Then, you have only yourself to blame. You can keep people from getting angry with you by keeping in mind the following:

- **Let people be who they are...**

People resent you if you point out their mistakes, if you tell them what to wear, how to act. They don't want you to try to change their behavior. They will get angry if you barge in without being invited, ask too many personal questions, talk down to them, demand to know about their every move, or make unreasonable demands on their time.

Your teenage son may dress very sloppy when he invites his friends to the house, but he is not hurting you. It is better not to say anything to him about it. He will resent being told to change his clothes or being criticized for his appearance. Making an issue about it can even result in his becoming rebellious.

The only time it is appropriate to tell people about their behavior is when it really interferes with your life. If your son dresses sloppy to go to a restaurant with you, and you feel upset about being seen with him, you can say something. He can be given the choice to change or stay home.

When you are not adversely affected by the way people behave, you have to let them be whoever they are, especially if they are important to you. That may mean overlooking their imperfections. If they do something that annoys you, it might be better to keep quiet or walk away.

People have a right to be treated as well as you want to be treated by them. All of them, even small children, have a right to respect. They are less likely to be angry with you when you treat them as human beings.

■ **Be consistent...**

People don't like it if you give them support one minute and then later criticize them.

Lynn, 28, was dating Paul. He made her angry by giving her mixed messages. He told her he loved her, but he never seemed to want to see her more than once a week. When they met, he said flattering things to her, but was always vague about when they would get together again. He acted loving, but said they were not to consider themselves a couple. Lynn realized that Paul might be terrified of commitment, but she was still angry and confused.

Violet, 41, made the man she was living with angry by being affectionate one minute, and furious at him the next. At those times, she acted like she hated him. He could accept her anger, but not her way of showing it.

If you usually behave like these people, you have to work on being consistently loving.

■ **Show your vulnerability...**

There is nothing wrong in showing confidence and being proud of yourself, but there is a lot wrong with flaunting your successes, never admitting you are wrong or have flaws, and acting like you don't need anyone. Let people know that you do need them because you have fears. They will be relieved and glad to learn that you are vulnerable, and will probably feel more comfortable with you.

■ **Take responsibility for your actions...**

You infuriate people if you say things like "if it wasn't for you, I could.." or "you made me do that...". Don't blame them when you do something. If someone is angry because you have criticized him, made unreasonable demands, or have been abusive, you make him even angrier when you deny it. Let him know when he is right.

■ **Be forgiving...**

Stop holding grudges. You put extra stress on your body when you make a mental tally of all the things you see someone do wrong. You get him furious if you keep reminding him of what he did in the past. Live in the moment and deal with something when it happens, and then forget about it. When someone does something that upsets you, tell him you are angry and then let it go. No one likes to have the past thrown in his face and used as a weapon later on to humiliate him.

■ **Be more positive...**

If you walk around with a frown and an angry look, or only express negative feelings, your negative energy can breed negative energy in others. People don't want to be dragged down and may blame you if you have that effect on them. Work on having a more positive outlook. People gravitate toward those who are cheerful.

■ **Show your feelings...**

People won't like it if you never react to what they say or do. They may feel shut out, think you are not interested in them, that you don't care enough to share your feelings. They may be angry if you are always complaisant and agree to everything without really meaning it. They may be angry if you are always indecisive. People want to have their feelings acknowledged and get feedback when they are upset so they can feel validated.

If you act cool and detached, and then analyze what they say, they may think you find them foolish. If you are very shy and find it hard to talk to people and to show your feelings to them, be aware that they may misinterpret your silence and assume you think you are superior to them.

People are less likely to be angry with you if you react to them rather than being detached. If you are open and honest, they will probably accept what you say.

Seeing Hidden Anger

Some people are obviously angry: they are aggressive and yell at you, cut in front of you, blow their car horns at you, berate you, tell you what to do, or hit you. Others show their anger in more subtle ways: they manipulate you, cheat you, or try to outdo you.

Some other people are harder to figure out: they act agreeable, try very hard to please and are self-sacrificing, but below the surface, they are angry. How do you know when a person who never uses words to communicate is upset or angry? How can you deal with a child or an adult who has anger that you can't see?

If you look hard, you will see that a person's actions and body language reveal his true feelings. You can know he is angry, even if does not tell you in words, if you see that:

- His face shows a slight scowl.
- He fidgets rather than sitting perfectly still.
- He taps his toe or drums his fingers.
- He mutters under his breath.
- His voice sounds slightly annoyed.
- He seems cold and distant.

Reasons for Hiding Anger

There are many reasons a person may hold back on expressing his anger:

■ He is afraid you will hurt him...

Betsey said nothing when her husband did something she didn't like. She always found it hard to show her anger to anyone, but especially to him because he yelled at her for it. Even if she expressed a mild complaint, he got furious. Betsey felt intimidated and preferred to keep quiet.

Tina spent her life acting agreeable and overly nice, helping others and never asking for anything in return. She tiptoed around, especially at work. People there took advantage of her, ordered her around, sent her on errands, ignored her, or gave her poor reviews. She never complained or said anything.

As a child, Tina was ignored by her parents. She felt unimportant, but thought that if she did everything her parents wanted, she would get their approval. She even did extra things to be noticed, like scrubbing the bathroom. Tina had gone through life with that mindset, working overtime and being extra conscientious at her job to get the boss' approval.

The problem was that being good and nice had not prevented others from mistreating Tina, and she felt angry about it. But, like many passive people, Tina wanted approval from others and believed that she would be hurt if she showed her anger. So, she said nothing, but she was not being rewarded for keeping quiet.

You may have someone in your life who doesn't let you know when he is angry because he finds you too overbearing or judgmental. If he is like that with everyone, then you know that you are probably not to blame for his passivity. Otherwise, you have to look at how your behavior must change before he opens up. You cannot expect anyone to express his angry feelings if he gets censored for doing so.

■ **He is afraid his anger will hurt you...**

Some passive people who never express anger believe that if they did, they would be explosive or violent and they would hurt you. They don't really know what they are capable of because they have never had an opportunity to find out. Since they are probably afraid of being destroyed by your anger, they assume that you are afraid of theirs. They somehow think it is their mission in life to protect you. When they feel stronger and more able to defend themselves, they don't see other people as being so fragile.

Dealing With the Unexpressive Person

When you are with someone who does not express his feelings, especially his anger, the following guidelines may be helpful:

■ **Know what you feel...**

Try to figure out exactly what effect someone's silence has on you:

• Does being with him make you feel lonely?

• Are you angry that he doesn't share his feelings with you?

• Do you feel unimportant because he doesn't give you feedback on your ideas?

• Do you feel shut out by his silence?

• Do you feel frustrated when you can't figure him out?

• Do you feel sad about not knowing what he feels?

• Do you get nervous about his being easily hurt?

• Are you glad to be with him because you know he won't be verbally abusive to you?

- Do you feel like bullying him because he won't defend himself?

■ **Express your feelings...**

A passive person usually doesn't realize that he is important enough to have any impact on anyone else and that being quiet can make you upset or angry. So you have to tell him exactly at the moment it is happening. When you are clear about what you feel, you can then communicate these feelings to him. If you ask him for his opinion about something and he doesn't answer, you have to tell him you feel hurt or angry or scared about it.

■ **Encourage him to express his anger...**

Pearl was angry with her husband Jeff for never showing his feelings, especially his anger. She felt too alone in the relationship the way it was and wished Jeff would not act so controlled. She wanted him to disagree with her, even if he raised his voice to do it.

Jeff was quiet because that was what he was taught to be in his family, but also because he felt intimidated by Pearl. If he ever did disagree with her, she seemed so critical of him.

It would be better if Jeff expressed anger no matter how Pearl reacted, but he was waiting for her to be more encouraging.

If you are dealing with someone who does not communicate or is withdrawn, you need to understand that he may not even know what he is feeling. If you think he is angry, it can be helpful to tell him. Hearing his anger identified can put him in touch with it, and, if you are right, help him to express it.

Then, be sure you don't criticize him when he does. If you want someone to be more expressive, you have to make it safe for him to be. If he feels threatened, he will keep quiet.

If after all your effort to be patient and understanding with someone who has hidden anger he shows no interest in working on his relationship with you, you may have to leave. You may prefer to find others who are more verbal and expressive.

9. COPING WITH MANIPULATORS

Understanding the Behavior

You may not be passive-aggressive, but you will probably meet lots of people who are. This is the most common way that people express anger, and even people who are usually passive or aggressive can be passive-aggressive at times. This behavior is popular because it offers the passive-aggressive person so many benefits:

THE BEHAVIOR	THE REWARD
Helplessness: flaunting inadequacy and incompetence	• getting rescued by you • getting attention and concern from you • having an excuse to be irresponsible
Illness: playing up being sick, acting frail	• getting pity, attention from you
Defiance: doing the opposite of what you want	• getting negative attention • having control over you
Failure: fouling up work, school	• being taken care of • acting like a victim
Surprise: doing the unexpected	• putting you off guard to feel in control
Guilt: acting like a martyr	• preventing you from saying no
Bingeing or Starving	• upsetting you, feeling powerful

Being a Victim

You may be allowing someone to manipulate you because you get something from feeling like a victim.

Corey, 44, had a home-based business. He felt that his wife was taking advantage of his being home all day by leaving him with all the responsibilities of running a household and taking care of a family.

Although she did not have a job, she left every morning to go to various activities that interested her, including exercise classes, tennis, committee meetings. She often did not return until the evening.

Corey shopped for food, drove their two young children to activities, prepared meals, and cleaned the house. He complained to his wife that he thought it was unfair for him to do so much, but he continued to do it.

At the same time, Corey did nothing to discipline the children. When he was home with them, he gave them whatever they asked for and he let them do whatever they wanted. When his wife came home, she took charge and usually took those privileges away from them.

The arrangement certainly seemed one-sided, with Corey taking on the role that most women have had for years, staying at home with the chores and the children, while his wife took on the role many men have had, staying out and having fun.

Corey came to therapy sessions supposedly so he could stop taking on a victim role in relation to both his wife and his children. He felt they were taking advantage of him, but he never refused to do what any of them wanted. He turned off his anger and seemed resigned to his role as a caretaker.

In reality, it was not that simple. Despite feeling used and taken for granted, Corey actually did not want to give it up. There were too many things about it that he enjoyed:

- Corey liked being needed and feeling indispensable. He felt like a failure in life. He thought people did not like him, and he was not that successful in his career. Taking care of the children and the house gave Corey a purpose for existing.

- Corey liked feeling like a martyr and thinking of himself as suffering, just as his mother had. He had been close to her as a child and identified with her in many ways.

- Corey thought it was wrong to ask for anything for himself. He wanted his wife or children to give to him without his having to say anything, and anything they gave him because he demanded it would not be meaningful.

- Corey liked having an excuse for why he was not more successful in his work. He could tell himself it was because he was too busy being a caretaker.

Corey saw that what he was doing was filling a need, and was not anyone else's fault. He continued the behavior because he got something from it. If he did not want to stay home, he could refuse and insist that his wife take on more responsibilities. But then he would have to satisfy his desire to be needed in some other way. Perhaps he could have fitted in some volunteer job in a soup kitchen, a hospital for sick children, or a home for the elderly.

Are you allowing others to manipulate you because get some satisfaction from being in a victim position? If you are, fill in the following chart.

Make a list of any situations you are in that make you feel used, what benefits you derive from doing them, and other ways you can get those needs met.		
BEING A VICTIM		
Situation	Benefits	Alternatives

What have you learned about yourself from filling in this chart? Are you really being victimized? Are you in any situations because you enjoy the benefits? If so, it will be hard for you to get out of them unless you replace them with more constructive situations that still fulfill your needs.

What to Do

Do you want to avoid being manipulated by others? It may be

difficult at times because you may not realize that you are being manipulated. A passive-aggressive person can get you to do what he wants without your knowing it.

You can be more in control if you do the following:

■ **Identify the behavior as passive-aggressive...**

When you feel manipulated by someone, you can assume that what he is doing is passive-aggressive. It may be very difficult to be sure if you are right because he may have excuses that sound reasonable or that can be chalked up to coincidence. You may wonder whether his behavior is an act of hostility to get back at you, or whether he is doing something for his own purposes only.

Suppose your child doesn't do his homework and his grades go down. How do you know what that means? Maybe he doesn't understand the work and is too shy to ask for help. Maybe he is upset about something and can't concentrate on school. Maybe he is doing something else when he should be doing his homework. What if you question him and he tells you all these things are true? You still cannot rule out the possibility that he is purposely neglecting his work to upset you.

If someone doesn't even know that his behavior is passive-aggressive, how can you? You just have to trust your instincts. If you do you stand a better chance of not letting anyone manipulate you.

■ **Set limits on what you will do...**

Once you determine that someone's behavior is passive-aggressive, you have to decide if it bothers you. If it makes you feel used, you have a right to set limits on what you are willing to do and what you won't do. You don't have to be a victim.

If someone asks you to bail him out of trouble, drive him around, retrieve lost objects, or help him out in any other way, you may think doing it a few times is fine. If he asks you repeatedly and it gets to be a pattern, you might not want to continue to help him. When you keep coming to his aid, you reinforce his helplessness and his dependency on you, and you encourage him to continue to be passive-aggressive.

When you are clear about what you want from this person, tell him. Maybe you want him to leave you alone, or become more self-sufficient, or take better care of himself. It is also up to you to set limits and change them at any time, no matter what you have been doing previously. When he learns that you refuse to bail him out, he will give up the behavior and become more independent.

- **Encourage him to be direct...**

A person who is passive-aggressive is hiding his anger behind actions. He may not even know how to be more open. If you want him to stop the behavior and begin to use words instead, you have to tell him you won't put up with it any other way. This is especially true if you are dealing with a child. He has to learn to say what he feels. An adult may have to overcome a lifetime of expressing his anger in devious ways, but you can help by encouraging open expression.

People Who Deceive

Another way that people act out their anger with manipulation is by being deceptive. They try to use you, lie to you, mislead you, or betray you. They may be strangers, friends or family members. The fact that you are related doesn't stop them. They pretend to care about you and then they do something that hurts you.

The deceiver is an angry person who probably was rejected, ignored, criticized, or abandoned in childhood. He grew up believing that the only way to get ahead is to hurt others and use them. He manipulates you because he sees you as an enemy. He feels inadequate and only experiences a sense of power when he can impress you or get you to play by his rules.

You can be deceived in business dealings by a salesman who is only interested in making money. He may try to sell you a used car, an appliance, or any other product by falsely advertising it or promising more than he can deliver. He can tell you he lowered the price when he didn't, or tell you that it has features it does not. He may offer you his services and then try to charge you more than he originally said. He may agree on a price, but then do a much poorer job than he promised to do.

When the deceiver is someone close, it can be more upsetting than if he is a stranger. You can be betrayed by a lover who is unfaithful, by a friend who turns against you unexpectedly after you have been helpful, or by a family member who badmouths you to others behind your back.

Why It Makes You Angry

People deceive you because that is how they express their anger, and being deceived by them may make you angry for many reasons:

■ **You feel hurt...**

When someone important in your life deceives you, it can be very hurtful. You know that if that person cared about you, he wouldn't do something that was harmful to your welfare. His actions indicate his lack of caring and so you feel rejected and angry.

You can feel just as angry when you are deceived by a stranger. Even if he means nothing to you, you may still want to think he cares about you. When he tries to fool you and you see that he only cares about himself, you may feel hurt, then angry.

■ **You feel disappointed...**

You may feel disappointed in yourself for having such poor judgment and thinking this person was trustworthy; and for being so gullible and letting him deceive you.

You may feel disappointed in him for not being what you thought he was.

Protecting Yourself

How can you avoid being deceived by anyone? Most people are honest, but others are self-centered and do what they want to do, no matter how it may hurt you. How can you know who to trust?

If you cannot see through this kind of person, you become his victim. He is good at spotting who he can betray. You can't stop anyone from trying to deceive you, but you can become so wise that you see what he is doing and you refuse to be a part of it.

Whether you are dealing with a salesman, a family member, or anyone else, it helps to keep the following in mind:

■ **If you believe, he will deceive...**

Before Helen was married to her husband and they were dating,

*she thought he was charming, witty, generous, loving, and attentive.
After all, he bought her little gifts and said flattering things to her.*

*After they were married about a year, Helen's husband became
selfish, critical, and disinterested in her. She felt betrayed and angry.
She now realized that when they were dating, his behavior was all an
act to win her approval. After they got married, he felt it was safe to
turn off the charm.*

When Helen was dating her husband, she failed to see that her
husband was really very self-centered. He spent all of the time talking
about himself and never asked her about herself or where she wanted
to go. At the time, his bossiness seemed masterful and she thought he
was taking charge. Because she wanted to believe all was well when it
was not, she got carried away with the flattering things he said about
her. She created a fantasy about him and tuned out any behavior she
didn't like. She did not prepare herself to see him as he really was.

Just because someone is a high official, a famous movie actor, a
renowned scholar, or a millionaire, he is not immune to making false
claims. Many people with good reputations have turned out to be shams
and have taken advantage of others.

The person who deceives usually gives little signals that something
is not right. If you need to believe he is perfect, you glorify him and put
him up on a pedestal. You take everything he says at face value and tell
yourself he has virtues that he has not. You exaggerate his good
qualities, and when he exhibits something negative or manipulates you,
you find excuses or overlook it.

Everyone has faults and no one is perfect. It is important not to
make anyone into a god, but to see yourself as equal to him. You get
deceived when you are too trusting. You may assume everyone has
good intentions, would not hurt you, and means what they say. You
can't just give every person the benefit of the doubt. Many people will
place their needs above yours and will try to use you for their own gain.
It takes time to find out how honest someone is.

To protect yourself from hurt, ask a lot of questions about anything
you want to know and then pay close attention to the answers. Don't
let anyone use jargon without your asking him to explain what you don't
understand. If he says he is an expert, get him to prove it.

If you are being interviewed for a job, you have a right to question the interviewer. You need to ask what your salary is going to be, what benefits you can expect, what hours you have to work, how many vacation days you get, and what your exact duties will be. You need to be given an accurate job description. The interviewer will probably think more of you for asking so many questions, not less of you. It shows that you are in charge of your life.

If you ask no questions, you can easily be mislead. This is true about buying a product, too. You need to ask the salesman what the features are of each brand, how the price compares, and what kind of track record regarding durability each company has for its product. Then, you can make an intelligent choice, and not let him fool you with fast talking.

■ **Trust your intuition...**

You are the expert on your feelings, not someone who says he is. Only you can determine what is good or right for you.

Long before you see evidence that something is wrong, your intuition may tell you this person is conning you. In spite of his saying sensible things, his non-verbal behavior, such as avoiding eye contact or having a phony smile, may tell you he is lying. You have to go with what you feel more than what you know. By the time you find out the facts, it may be too late.

■ **Look at his manner...**

The person who betrays you usually has low self-esteem and expects to be ignored. He wants your approval, but he cannot believe that he will get it if you see him as he really is. He therefore puts on a front to impress you. That doesn't mean that everyone who does these things is out to deceive you. It does mean that everyone who is deceptive has this kind of manner. If you are ready to see it, you will.

• He acts charming, smiles a lot when he talks, and is friendly and cheerful. He seems warm and interested in you. He may look you in the eyes to convince you he has nothing to hide.

• He says things like *I promise you* or *trust me* to make you think he is interested in the best for you and that he will deliver it. He says these things, but he has no intention of following through with them.

• He uses flattery to butter you up and win you over. He tells you he admires your appearance, your accomplishments, your family, your good taste, or anything else he thinks will make you believe he is interested in you.

- He brags about himself, tells you he is an expert on whatever subject you discuss with him, even if he is not. If you are about to hire him for something, he tells you he is the best.
- He tells you things that may not be true.

Veronica, a teacher, married a man who told her when they met that he had a college degree when he did not. He lied to impress her because he thought she would not stay with him if she knew the truth. Of course, she was more upset about his lying than the fact that he had no degree.

The person who lies to you is afraid that if he is honest with you, you will see his weaknesses and reject him. He does not want you to know who he really is or what he really thinks. He tells you what he thinks you want to hear and he pretends to be the person he thinks you want him to be. He wants your approval so much that he lies to protect himself. What he fails to realize is that if you find out he is lying, you are more likely to reject him than if he tells the truth, no matter what it is.

You can catch the lies if you can spot the inconsistencies. What he says today may not match what he said yesterday. He may contradict himself even in the same sentence. His facial expression may not match the words he uses. He may sound friendly, tell you he cares about you, and look hostile. He may smile at you but not respond to anything you have said. He may tell you he is rich but seem to have limited possessions or be wary about spending money. He may make promises but not keep them.

■ Encourage honesty...

Sometimes, people lie to you because they think you will be upset by the truth or because you put them down for telling the truth. It is up to you to be open, and to let them know you prefer honesty at all costs.

Sylvia, 45, had been having an affair for a year. She thought about leaving her husband, but did nothing about it. He was very dependent on her in every way, had low self-esteem and few friends. She was afraid he would fall apart if she was not there for him.

Sylvia's husband suspected she was involved with someone and he confronted her. At first, she denied it. Finally, she did admit it, but he got very upset. So she told him it was over, even though it wasn't. Sylvia didn't want to be responsible for upsetting him, so she kept lying.

Sylvia was wrong to lie or be unfaithful, but she found it safer than confronting her husband. He showed that he could not handle the truth, even though he kept saying that is what he wanted. He used his fragility as a way to make her feel sorry for him and be tied to him. It did do that, but it also made her deceitful. She might have been more truthful if he seemed stronger or acted as though he really wanted to hear it.

- ### Get everything in writing...

If you have any business dealings with anyone, even a friend or a relative, put all agreements and terms in a written statement signed by both of you. Have it include exactly what happens if the other person pulls out. Then, no one can claim you said something that you didn't or insist it was never said when it was. Oral agreements are completely subject to memory, which can be highly inaccurate.

- ### Get a life...

If you realized your partner was a fraud, would you still be involved with him? You might want to be if you had no friends and so were desperate. Unless you put your eggs in more than one basket, that is, have several people in your life who matter to you, you become too dependent on one person. Then, you may stay with him no matter how he treats you.

You also need to get out into the world and mix with lots of people. You can do that by working, joining organizations, and traveling. You soon see that there are many kinds of people in the world, some of whom are straightforward and decent, and some of whom are dishonest or are manipulators. You become adept at picking out the ones who are out to con you. You become tough.

When you stay home by yourself or with one or two other people, you can easily be too naive about the rest of the world and too trusting. If you feel inadequate, you want approval from everyone, and you fall prey to those who pretend to care about you. When you have a full life, you are not so easily fooled.

■ **Get help...**

If you find that you always allow others to betray you, or you seem to gravitate toward people who use you, consider seeing a professional counselor. You may need to work on improving your self-image and on becoming more discriminating.

10. COPING WITH AGGRESSIVE PEOPLE

Reasons for Aggression

You probably have dealt with aggressive people, and you may live with them. You may have been spoken to rudely by a clerk in a store; have blown your horn at a driver who cut in front of you and been given a finger; or you may have a boss who is arrogant and intimidating, criticizes everything you do, talks to you as though he is superior, and never admits to being wrong about anything.

You could feel intimidated by these people, unless you realize that you don't have to take their behavior personally. Usually, their aggression is not about you, but rather about issues they have not resolved. They probably mistreat other people too.

A person may be aggressive for many reasons:

- **He expects you to hurt him...**

When someone is aggressive, there is a strong possibility that he was verbally or physically abused as a child and he now expects to be hurt by everyone he meets. To protect himself, he may become critical, controlling, or violent, and develop a defensive attitude no matter how you treat him. The driver who acts hostile exaggerates the danger and feels threatened by you. He sees you as an enemy out to get him.

When someone close to you acts aggressive, it may be because he misinterprets your words and hears them as an attack. He anticipates being hurt by you, so he thinks he hears hostility in your innocent comments or in your tone of voice. He may read something personal into everything you do. If you burn the toast, spill something, or have a car accident, he may say you did it to upset him and not believe your explanation.

A person close to you may feel very safe about being aggressive when he is with you, but doing so probably gets him the rejection that he is trying to avoid, and not the love he so desperately craves.

- **He feels powerless...**

Usually, an aggressive person is really someone who feels weak in relation to others. He does things he doesn't want to do because he cannot say no to someone. Then he blames that person for making him do them.

When the frustration and anger build up, he may stop being passive and go to the opposite extreme of screaming and yelling or using curse words. He may then say things in the heat of rage that sound hateful, like he was a child having a temper tantrum. He may not be able to clearly communicate in words that he feels scared, and you may misunderstand his actions. This can make him more furious.

- **He feels inferior...**

A person who bullies others seems overbearing and even scary, but he probably acts that way because he has a poor self-image. He cannot tolerate his imperfections and does not expect you to tolerate them either. He feels inadequate and does not believe you will pay any attention to him. He becomes loud, intrusive, critical, and intimidating to stop you from ridiculing him.

If your boss is aggressive, it could be because he is reporting to a superior who is bullying him, and he could be taking his frustrations out on you. He could see you as more competent than him, more experienced, or better able to get along with others, so he could be jealous, and afraid you will take over his job unless he keeps you in your place.

- **He has no boundaries...**

Many people are aggressive because they are too wrapped up in themselves to see that other people exist. They want a lot of attention, and they do whatever they please to get it. Emotionally, they are on the level of a young child who does not know that you are separate and have your own needs. They put no boundary between themselves and you, so they feel free to invade your space. Like that young child, they barge in, say inappropriate things, make demands, tug at you, and speak out of turn.

- You may have a neighbor you hardly know who frequently shows up at your door for a visit without first calling you, or who calls often to borrow some piece of equipment.

- You may have a relative who calls and says he is coming to stay for a while, without asking you if you mind. He then makes constant demands to eat only certain foods and to keep the room a certain temperature. He keeps you up when you want to go to sleep.

- You may work with someone who always asks you personal questions and doesn't give up if you refuse to answer her. If she gossips about other coworkers, you know she tells them about you.

- You may have a friend who interrupts you when you are out to dinner with other people and talking to them. It could be that he wants everyone to focus on him and so he hardly listens to what anyone else has to say.

- You may have met someone at a party who stands very close to you and taps you on your shoulder when he talks to you.

Coping with Abuse

People who behave in the ways described may not even realize that their behavior is intrusive and annoying. You may have to point it out to them. If you can do it without being attacking, they may be willing to treat you better. If not, you can only try to avoid them, if possible, or at least have as little to do with them as you can.

It is much more difficult to deal with someone whose aggression is much more extreme and can be considered abusive. You may have a family member who gets out of control, yells and calls you hurtful names when he is angry. Even if he never hits you, his verbal abuse may have the same negative effect on you as if it were physical.

No matter why someone is abusive, he has no right to hurt you, and you don't have to let him. You have a better chance of resisting his abuse if you can keep the following ideas in mind:

■ **See the abuser for what he is...**

A bully may insult you and say hateful things. He may say it is your fault that he is angry. The important thing in dealing with an abusive person is not to take him literally. Don't automatically assume that what he says to you in the heat of his rage is true or has anything to do with you. If you do, you get caught up in feeling attacked, in feeling sorry for yourself, and maybe in being afraid of him.

You don't have to forgive him if he insults you, but neither should you be in awe of him or to see him as powerful. He may look and act like a powerful monster, but he may really be like a scared little child.

Rita had spent many years being abused by her husband Joe before they both came for counseling. Whenever he was angry with her, he became furious and hit her. Rita never knew what might set him off.

As a child, Rita was terrified of her father. He yelled at her and slapped her when he didn't like something she did. To protect herself, she often hid from him. As an adult, she was just as afraid of Joe's temper. She hesitated to talk to him and tried to avoid him most of the time. When he was angry, she tried to get away from him.

Joe had been ignored by his parents as a child and felt hurt when Rita shut him out. He covered that hurt by bullying and scaring her. Then she retreated more, which got Joe more furious. Rita's way of protecting herself against Joe's aggression thus led to more of it.

To Rita, both men were scary and seemed like giants. In reality, they were both short and thin. They both compensated for their inadequacy feelings by dominating her. When Rita was a child, her father was much bigger than her, and much more powerful, despite his short stature. There was not much she could do to protect herself.

As an adult, however, Rita did not see herself or her husband realistically. She was certainly equal in size to him, and almost as powerful. Inside, he was not the strong person that she saw, nor was she as helpless as she labeled herself. She did not realize she could stand up to him and demand that he stop.

Rita needed to know that Joe was aggressive mostly because he was feeling rejected, and that he was not a monster but an insecure, vulnerable man who wanted to be loved. Joe had to learn to express his anger in words, and to be more loving if he wanted to receive love.

When you are faced with someone who is abusive to you, look between the lines of what he says and does and see his fear of being abandoned and of not being loved. Try to see that he feels inadequate and tries to cover it by being abusive. Realize that you may be dealing with someone who is very immature and self-centered. When you see him for what he is, you may be able to hold on to who you are.

■ **Encourage communication...**

When someone is enraged and is having a temper tantrum, you can refuse to respond. Whether you are dealing with a young child who kicks you or screams when he is angry, or an adult who curses, yells, throws things, or hits you when he is angry, you can insist he talk to you instead, and then be sure not to criticize what he says.

■ **Be assertive...**

If someone makes inappropriate physical contact with you or asks personal questions, let him know he is invading your space. If he is being abusive by screaming at you, demand to be treated well. Often, a person who is out of control is unable to stop himself and it scares him. He wants you to stop him, and is relieved when you tell him you won't put up with it. He likely has more respect for you than if you say nothing.

Make sure that you make your demands in an assertive way. Don't stoop to anyone's level of name-calling or hitting to show him what he is doing. He will just resent you and do it more, and he may be better at it than you. You also probably won't feel good about yourself if you act aggressive.

■ **If the abuse is physical, get help...**

If someone is beating you, he is committing a crime, and you need to report it to the police. Unfortunately, they may not do anything until you are actually hurt.

Before that happens, look in the phone book for a center for those who are battered, and consider staying there for a while. Many women, especially, have been stalked and sometimes killed by the person who was abusing them when they tried to leave or they reported him.

Don't delude yourself into thinking that this person is going to change, no matter what promises he makes to you. Unless he gets intensive counseling, he will continue to be out of control when he is angry.

■ **Look for substance abuse...**

Before you take the blame for someone's verbal or physical abuse, see if drugs or alcohol are contributing to his being aggressive. Most violence is committed while someone is using drugs and alcohol because they change brain chemistry, cloud judgment, loosen inhibition, and often intensify anger levels. They make someone more violent than he would be without them.

If you suspect drinking or using drugs is making someone you care about violent, try to get him into a treatment program. If it is true about someone who is not important to you, try to avoid dealing with him.

■ **Remove yourself...**

When you are dealing with a friend, a lover, a family member, or a business person who is aggressive, you don't have to let him mistreat you. If you are being abused and nothing changes after you stand up to him, find ways to get away from him. In a work situation, complain to the Human Resources person or, if you have to, quit your job. In a family situation, if professional counseling doesn't work, move away or file for divorce.

Abusive Parents

Any treatment by a parent that does not encourage you to be yourself, express your feelings, and make your own decisions, and does not include more emotional support and recognition than criticism or other negative feedback can be considered abusive. Was one or both of your parents abusive? What kind of abuse did you get? Was it any of the following?

■ **Verbal abuse...**

Did you have a parent who hurt your feelings with insulting words? Were many of your actions criticized? Were you called names, such as stupid or lazy? Did you deserve the names you were called? Do you ever call yourself these names now?

■ **Physical abuse...**

Were you beaten or slapped by one of your parents? What was it for? Were you given any reason for it? The majority of parents love their children, but some express their anger in a way that seems like they don't. If you were abused by a parent, you may have a hard time not taking it personally or believing there was any love there.

- **Mixed messages...**

Did your abusive parent call you names or yell at you one day, and then later or the next day treat you with affection or praise? Did he beat you one minute and hug you the next or later act as though it never happened? Did he treat you badly and then later apologize, only to repeat the pattern soon after? Did he criticize you to your face but say positive things about you to other people?

Which message did you believe? Did you think the positive behavior was a pretense and only believe the negative? Did you think he only apologized or acted loving because he felt guilty about being abusive?

Criticism is more powerful than praise, so it is easy to forget or discount praise when it comes. Do you have difficulty now believing people when they are nice to you? When you meet people, do you initially distrust them?

How does a parent who spews hateful words at his child one minute and is loving the next really feel? He probably has love for the child, but when he hates what the child does, he acts like he hates the child himself. His anger can be brief, but while it is rage, he feels hate. When the rage subsides, he again feels love.

- **Lack of praise and attention...**

Bernice was an only child, and, as both of her parents worked when she was growing up, she was frequently on her own. She made her own breakfast and lunch, came home from school every day to an empty house, and often found dinner left for her in the refrigerator. Her parents never seemed to have time for her and acted as though they forgot she existed.

Bernice received little feedback. Her parents expected her to do well in school, so they never praised her when she did. As a result, Bernice grew up to believe she was not very important or special. She didn't trust her intuition or her judgment. She also was shy and never learned to interact with others, so she never knew that she could have an effect on anyone.

Bernice's parents were not trying to be abusive and they did not realize how their behavior impacted on her. They were just too busy with their own lives to have a child. Unfortunately for Bernice, she didn't understand that when she was a child, and she felt abused.

Is your story similar? Did you have a parent who took you for granted? Who only spoke to you when you did something wrong? Who ignored you if you accomplished something? Sometimes it is worse to have your parents ignore you and never praise you than to have them angry and criticize you. At least when they act abusive they acknowledge your existence.

Are you able to praise yourself? Can you accept praise from others? If not, does it seem to stem from not being praised as a child?

■ **Control...**

Did your parents tell you what to do, how to think, where to go, and how to live your life? Did they have all kinds of rules for living? Were you given the freedom to express anger, fear, or sadness, or were you shot down when you did? Did you feel stifled by one of them?

A young woman felt smothered by her mother until she was able to move out. Her mother watched every move she made, was always concerned about her health and her safety, whether she was too warm or too cold, too hungry or too tired. She knew her mother loved her, but she had no privacy or sense of being a separate person when she was with her.

It is not likely this woman's mother thought she was being abusive by being so controlling, even though it felt that way to her daughter.

Don't Take It Personally

How can you not take it personally if one of your parents abused you? Only by understanding that the reasons have much more to do with him than with you. He brought his background with him and often interacted with his children in the same way that his parents treated him. This was probably not a conscious decision, but was the result of not having worked through the feelings he had about having been abused in childhood.

Here are some possible reasons your parent may have been abusive. See which seem to be true for your family history:

■ **He was immature....**

One young couple was married a few months when she became pregnant. They hadn't planned on becoming parents so soon, but they had the baby because they didn't believe in abortion.

Unfortunately, the baby was difficult. He cried often and slept little. They resented his intrusion on their time, so they were angry with him whenever he cried. When he was a toddler, he touched everything, and they were even more upset. They just didn't have the patience to be parents, and were not ready to cope with the needs of a child.

If that is how it was with your parents, keep in mind that you did not cause them to treat you the way they did. They were not reacting to you as an individual, but rather to their having to take care of you.

■ **His own upbringing got in the way...**

Was one or both of your parents brought up by a family that took attributes and accomplishments for granted and never gave him praise? Did that parent fail to praise you because he felt uncomfortable doing so? You cannot assume he didn't think you were fine just because he never said you were.

If you had a parent who felt inadequate, he may have considered your imperfections as a reflection on himself. That could have made him controlling, rigid, and overbearing. If he had an investment in making you succeed, he may have been angry if you got less than top grades in school. If he was overly concerned about what other people would think of your behavior, he may have constantly watched you. If he did not live a satisfying life when he was younger, he may have needed you to do better than him. If he tried to live through you, he may have been possessive and smothering.

If your parent did any of these things, try to find out from him or from a relative what happened to him when he was growing up that might have led to his style of parenting.

■ **He was jealous...**

Karen's mother was hostile to her, and whenever Karen talked to her father, her mother interrupted them. When he was not around, she told Karen negative things about him.

Karen felt abused by her mother as a child. As an adult, she saw that her mother had resented Karen's getting more attention from her father than her mother did.

In counseling, Karen realized that she was not responsible for making her mother jealous, and that the problem was between her mother and father. She didn't have to stop being friends with her father to please her mother.

When Selena was a little girl, people said she was pretty and gave her a lot of attention. Her mother, though, made critical remarks about her hair or her nose or her body. Later, when Selena got attention from boys, her mother told her she was fat. She also insinuated that Selena was sleeping with any boy she dated.

Selena's mother was always overweight, and was competitive about her appearance. She had grown up with negative messages about her looks, then married a man who had affairs with other women. She seemed to consider Selena's beauty and sexuality to be a threat, so she did all she could to take them away.

Unfortunately, Selena took everything her mother said personally. She always felt guilty about looking better than her mother, so she convinced herself that she was fat and ugly. She was never happy with her looks, even though her husband thought her very attractive. She also was unable to enjoy sex because she had picked up distortions about it from her mother.

It took a lot of counseling for Selena to separate her mother's messages from reality and see herself as she really was, not as her mother saw her.

■ He felt unappreciated...

If your father abused you, it may be that he was angry with your mother taking him for granted or ignoring him, he was afraid to tell her, and he took his anger out on you. It may be that he felt neglected by you and was angry with you for it. His anger about that may have been valid, or it may have been a distortion based on unrealistic expectations.

■ He had other problems...

Sylvia's mother was an alcoholic. When she drank, she had sudden fits of rage, screamed at Sylvia and shouted insults. Sometimes, she lost control and hit her. Her father was distant and passive, and although he was never hurtful, he never stopped the abuse.

Sylvia's mother should have been treated for alcoholism, but she wasn't. Sylvia partly blamed her father for this. She also thought his silence meant he condoned the treatment Sylvia got from her mother. Sylvia didn't know why she was being abused, but she believed it must be her fault.

In counseling, she learned that it had nothing to do with her. Her mother had a lot of frustrations in her life which led to her drinking: Sylvia's father was frequently unemployed, she didn't work, so there was little money; he was withdrawn and probably depressed, never wanted to go anywhere, and paid little attention to her.

If you got mistreated by a parent who drank or used drugs, or who had emotional problems, you have no way of knowing how he would have behaved if things had been different for him.

■ **You were similar to him...**

Many parents dislike certain traits in themselves, such as procrastinating or making poor choices. They then have no tolerance for the same trait in anyone else, especially their offspring. You may have been picked on by the parent you most resemble, either in appearance or personality. All that means is you reminded this parent of what he didn't like in himself.

■ **Your behavior was intolerable...**

All of these examples are about problems your parent had that were not caused by you. It is possible, though, that you did do something that increased his anger. Did you give him a hard time in any way? Were you rebellious and uncooperative? Did you take drugs, cut classes, have wild friends, get arrested or run away from home? Why did you do these things? Was it in reaction to the way this parent treated you? Which came first? Was it a vicious cycle of anger from your parent, then irritating behavior on your part, then more anger from him?

You may have behaved in unacceptable ways to get back at an abusive parent, which is understandable. Nevertheless, if you acted out your anger and hurt in destructive ways, you have to take responsibility for making the situation worse.

Changing the Messages

You deserved to be treated well, and you have a right to be angry that you weren't. No matter what problems your parent had, or how you behaved, he should not have been abusive. Instead of telling yourself that you are entirely to blame for the abuse you got, that you deserved it, and that you failed at being a good son or daughter, or that your parent was rotten, consider the following:

- **He loved you in his way...**

If your parent criticized you, it doesn't mean that he didn't love you or that he meant what he said. He may have been critical because he loved you. The love could have made him care too much about what you did. If he wanted you to be happy all of the time, he found it painful when you weren't. It created anxiety for him, and then he blamed you for being the cause of his anxiety. He probably didn't know how to be helpful to you when you were hurting, and frustration about it could have caused him further anger.

If he wanted you to stay in his life, he may have tried to hold on to you by being controlling and possessive.

He may have done everything wrong, but he may not have been capable of doing more. If he had personal problems, they may have interfered with his being a better parent. If he never got help for it, he may not have had the tools to change his behavior.

- **You could not have stopped the abuse....**

There is no use saying *if only I had..., he would have treated me better*. The fact is that an abusive parent cannot stop what he is doing without professional help. Trying to please him doesn't work. Do something right and he finds something else to criticize. Standing up to him might help when you are an adult, but when you were a child, it could have made him treat you worse.

Even if your behavior sometimes angered him, you are not responsible for his being abusive. There are many ways a person can verbalize his anger without resorting to rage or violence.

Part Four

MAKING POSITIVE CHANGES

This section shows you how to make changes in your thinking and your behavior in order to be less angry at yourself and at others. These include loving yourself, becoming assertive, seeing alternatives, become more independent, having more fun, and slowing down.

11. BEING LESS ANGRY AT YOURSELF

Test Your Self-Esteem

Look at the following chart to see how much confidence you have:

Check off whether you do any of the following:

☐ I blame myself when others mistreat me.

☐ I blame myself when others make a mistake or do something foolish.

☐ I stay in relationships with people who criticize me and mistreat me.

☐ I have very high expectations for myself.

☐ I blame myself when I make a mistake.

☐ I compare myself to others in looks, money, family, job, achievements, etc.

☐ I usually think I am inferior to others.

☐ I apologize for my angry feelings, say I am sorry.

☐ I believe it is true when people criticize me.

☐ I dislike many of my traits, such as being lazy or shy.

☐ I do self-destructive things, like overeating, using drugs, drinking, gambling.

☐ I need approval from everyone.

☐ I cannot tolerate faults in others.

☐ I procrastinate and avoid starting things.

☐ I need to win and get angry with myself if I lose.

☐ I must be the best and feel like a failure when I am not.

☐ I always think others are judging my actions and appearance.

☐ I assume they don't like me.

☐ I feel responsible when others are unhappy.

If you checked most of the statements, you probably need to work on raising your self-esteem. There is a direct correlation between your self-image and how angry you get or how you handle anger from other people. The more confidence you have, the less you take things personally and the more objective you can be.

When your self-esteem is low, you become dependent on love and acceptance from other people and what they think of you becomes very important. You take everything they do personally and easily feel hurt if you think they seem disinterested in you.

The worse your self-image, the more you believe people want to hurt you. Then, you interpret everything they do as an attack. It makes no difference what they really are doing. It may be innocent; it may be insignificant; it may be for your benefit. The lower your self-esteem, the more your perceptions may be distorted. As a result, you may be angry a lot of the time.

If your self-esteem is low, you may allow people to mistreat you. If you initially feel angry when someone hurts you, having low self-esteem can make you question your feelings or decide that you deserve the abuse. It takes confidence to demand better treatment.

You can see that if you want to stop taking everything personally and relate to other people with much less anger, it is crucial to have good self-esteem. When you can accept your imperfections and forgive your mistakes, you will be much less angry and less easily hurt by others.

Raising Your Self-Image

■ **Change your internal messages...**

Did you get negative messages from one or both parents? Do you fall apart when you get them from anyone now? Your feelings of self-worth come from your early years with your family. If you were praised when you were a child, you have a better chance at recovering quickly when someone criticizes you than if you did not get treated well.

John's low self-esteem developed as he was growing up. His father had ignored him, and his mother had been too self-centered to cater to his needs. She resented his need for attention and his saying no to her demands.

John tried rebelling in his teens, but his parents were so angry that he soon gave up and withdrew. He grew up thinking that he was a burden and that his needs made others unhappy.

As an adult, John felt deserving of any mistreatment he received from his boss, his wife, or anyone else he encountered. John's self-image reflected the negative attitude his parents seemed to have about him when he was a child.

When your self-esteem is low, you keep it that way by giving yourself negative messages. It takes a long time to stop being angry with yourself. You have to make a conscious effort to replace the old destructive internal messages with ones that are more realistic:

Old Message: **I must be loved by everyone.**
New Message: **I cannot make everyone love me, but I will survive.**

No matter what you do, you cannot be loved by everyone. There is no magic formula to make it happen, no right way to behave that guarantees popularity or acceptance by everyone. Even if you are very giving and agreeable, not everyone will think it is wonderful. Some people will be annoyed and think you are a wimp, and some will even be envious and feel threatened. What matters is that the people you care about love you.

If you accept the fact that you will never have everyone's approval, you won't get so angry or upset when people reject you.

Old Message: **My self-worth is based on what others think of me.**
New Message: **What I think of myself is more important than what others think.**

If you base your self-worth on what others think, then you allow criticism from one individual to overshadow praise from one hundred others. Since you can never get everyone to agree about your value, you cannot say who is right or wrong. When you have a low opinion of yourself, you teach others to think less of you. When you value yourself, you are able to ignore any criticism and not be dragged down by it.

You have to realize that people are not focused on you as much as they are on themselves. While you are worrying about what they are thinking about you, they are just as concerned about what you are thinking of them. They need approval too. They want you to like them, and if they are watching you, it is probably to see how you are sizing them up.

It is also true that other people are reacting in terms of their own needs, opinions, and idiosyncrasies much more often than they are reacting to you. What they say or do has more to do with them than it has to do with you. It is somewhat grandiose to believe that everyone has nothing better to do than to focus on you.

Old Message: **My self-worth depends on what I achieve.**
New Message: **Who I am is separate from what I do or what I own.**

You may have a lot of money because you inherit it, win a lottery, have good connections, successfully invest it, or find a job that pays well. You may be poor because you lose your job, have bad luck, or lack the appropriate skills.

Who you are is not defined by your income, your job, your title, your marital status, or your educational level. These factors are external and do not make you a better or worse person. What makes you unique is your values, ethics, beliefs, and feelings; your way of relating to others; your knowledge; your habits; and your past history. Your inner core stays the same all of the time, no matter whether or not your level of functioning changes because of illness, aging, or unforeseen events. That means that you remain worthwhile even if your external situation becomes worse.

Old Message: **I must be worthless if my mother or father said so.**
New Message: **My critical parent was wrong about me.**

When you were growing up, was one of your parents much more supportive than the other? Were you criticized much more by one than by the other? If so, how did you decide which one was right? Did you only believe the parent who said negative things about you and discard the positive messages you got from the other one?

Do you now put yourself down the way your critical parent did? Do you instead, praise yourself the way your supportive parent did? Unfortunately, it is common for people to discount any praise they receive when they also get criticism and abuse.

It may be time to consider that the parent who praised you was right and the one who hurt you was wrong, so you can base your self-image on positive messages. What others think of you may be distorted by their own problems. They may be critical of you because they cannot accept traits that they see in themselves, or because you remind them of someone who was abusive to them in the past.

Old Message: **It is my fault if someone is unhappy.**
New Message: **I am not responsible for making others happy.**

Nell was a teacher and often had to do paperwork in the house at night. Her husband wanted her to sit with him while he watched television. When Nell said she wasn't available, her husband felt rejected. He then turned his hurt feelings into attacks on her, telling her she was uncaring and mean.

Nell believed her husband was right about her, and she felt guilty and blamed herself for upsetting him. The fact is she was not to blame for her husband's hurt feelings or for his anger. She was not in a position to do what was best for him at this time, but he chose to believe otherwise. When Nell realized it was unfair of him to expect her to place his needs above hers when her job was at stake, she stopped berating herself about it.

In another situation, a young man named Joseph also took the blame where there was none. He was very shy and found it hard to speak when he was in the presence of more than one person. He was convinced that nothing he had to say was valuable and that no one would want to hear it.

Joseph went on a bus trip with some people he worked with and hardly said a word the whole day. Some of the people noticed and asked him what was wrong. One person seemed annoyed, which made him very uncomfortable. When he got home, Joseph was angry with himself for ruining everyone's day by being so quiet.

There was no way that the other people could actually have been that affected by how much Joseph talked to them. That idea was in his head. Although Joseph saw himself as unimportant and unequal to others, he also believed that he was powerful enough to affect their happiness.

Do you usually think it is your fault when someone is upset? Do you believe that it is up to you to make people happy, rather than their being responsible for their own happiness? That would mean that you have much more influence over others than you do.

Most of the time, people are angry or hurt because of reasons that have nothing to do with you. You cannot make them behave the way they do, and it is grandiose to think you can.

- **Appreciate your good qualities...**

Why did your partner pick you? What do the people in your life like about you? If you don't know, maybe you should ask them. What do you like about yourself? What qualities are you glad you have? Are you honest, caring, creative, dependable, perceptive, or sensitive? Do you have a good sense of humor? Do you take those qualities for granted because you think everyone has them? Unfortunately, many people don't and are dishonest, selfish, irresponsible, or insensitive. If you are not, you deserve to praise yourself for it.

Do you consider yourself intelligent? What is your criteria for evaluating your intelligence? Is it whether or not you went to college? how many degrees you have? how fast you read? how many facts you remember? Maybe you don't score high on any of these and so you think you are not smart.

Being good at details and the acquisition of facts is having left-brained intelligence. There is another kind of intelligence based on being right-brained and very intuitive. That makes you "street smart" instead of "book smart", but it doesn't make you less intelligent.

Are you comfortable thinking good things about yourself? Were you taught that you are supposed to be modest? The problem with hiding your assets from yourself is that other people may then see you as a loser. When you can appreciate your good qualities, you begin to feel and to act more confident.

- **Recognize your achievements...**

Never mind what you see other people achieve, or what you can't do and wish you could. Give yourself credit for even your smallest achievement. Don't take anything you do for granted. For instance, if you have trouble with tasks that involve mathematics and you suddenly are able to balance your checkbook, pat yourself on the back for it. If you are afraid to drive somewhere and then you do it, be proud of yourself. Give yourself credit for any improvement you make in your appearance, your income, your personality, your knowledge, or any other factors you consider important.

■ **Do what you do well...**

What talents and skills do you have? Do you excel at sports or painting or languages? Are you good with details or with people? Are you a good mother or a good friend? What are the skills that make you good at those roles? Is it being a good listener, being caring, supportive? Your ability to do something well can be the result of inherited talent, a strong interest, or acquired knowledge.

When you are not good at something, it could be because you are not interested in it. Instead of saying "I can't" about something you don't do well, try saying it is because "I don't want to". If it really bothers you that you don't have a particular skill, make it your business to learn it. You may discover abilities you didn't know you had.

You don't have to be good at everything. Pick those things you enjoy and do well, and use them as the guide for a career and for leisure activities. If you work well with people, pick a service career. If you are better at details, choose a field in which you can use equipment or figures. When you put yourself in situations where you can succeed, you have less reason to be angry with yourself.

■ **Accept your limitations...**

Are you angry with yourself for having any personality trait that you consider imperfect, such as being lazy, selfish, unassertive, angry, boring, or foolish? Do you think having any of these traits makes you worthless? Can you accept yourself, even if you make a mistake, overeat and gain weight, procrastinate, lose things, hurt someone's feelings? After you do something, do you say "I should have...", "I shouldn't have...", or "If only I had..."? Do you call yourself stupid?

When you make a mistake, do you think it means you are a failure? Since it is impossible not to make mistakes, it would be better to view them as teaching you something. For instance, if you get lost while driving, you have learned which streets to avoid next time. If you take your car to be repaired and you get charged too much, you have learned which garage to avoid the next time you need one.

No one can have perfect behavior at all times. If anything you do is not really harmful to you or to other people, stop worrying about it, and stop hating yourself for it. You are just human like everyone else. However, there is almost no behavior that cannot be changed. With the help of a professional counselor, you could learn to be more organized, to procrastinate less, to stop overeating, or even to be more caring.

■ **Set realistic standards...**

Arlene went on a diet in November and gave herself the deadline of her daughter's wedding in May to lose forty pounds. When the day came, she had lost thirty pounds, and instead of feeling good about it, she felt terrible because it was not forty. As long as her original goal was not reached, Arlene believed she was a failure.

The same thing happened to her brother when he thought about quitting smoking. He had smoked for thirty years, but in December he decided he would quit by the beginning of the new year. Just at that time, he had a lot of stress and did not quit. Instead of going forward to try again, he was so disappointed in himself that he gave up on ever quitting.

If these people had set more realistic standards for themselves, they would not have let themselves down. They needed to stop seeing things as all or nothing, and give themselves credit for the in-betweens, or at least try again.

If you are frequently disappointed and angry with yourself for not meeting certain goals, it may be that those goals are too high. Then, no matter what you do, you feel like a failure. Maybe you would have to be perfect to achieve them. When your goals are realistic, you are able to achieve them, and that helps your self-esteem.

You cannot always be the winner or be the best or have the most. Only one person can be that at any time. If you have a talent or a skill that makes you outstanding, you can aspire to greatness. You may become a recognized actor, musician, writer, political leader, or even a billionaire. If your abilities are average, it is unrealistic to expect this, and doing so will only lead to disappointment and anger.

That doesn't mean you can't be proud of yourself. If your goals are realistic, meaning they are appropriate to your level of ability, you can be thrilled when you reach them. Never mind what others have done. It is what you do that has to matter to you.

■ **Compare yourself only to yourself...**

Do you compare your looks, your income, your car, your house, and your children to how you were in the past or to other people? Do you usually think that others have more than you? Do you think they are smarter or happier?

Do you ever believe that some people could envy you? No matter what you have, there will always be people who have more than you, but there will also be people who have less. Do you always have to be the best or have the most? Are you ever satisfied if you come out equal to other people?

It may be that you are not the best judge of how you stand compared to others, since your evaluation may be distorted by a negative self-image. Successful people can feel poor; thin people can think they are fat; beautiful people can think they are ugly.

If you think everyone else is more confident or happier, you may be making false assumptions about them. Many people are able to put up a front and fool you into thinking they are happy when they are not. Unless you actually see for yourself what is going on or ask them yourself, you cannot really know.

When you compare yourself to others, your self-esteem can suffer. In order not to be angry with yourself, try comparing what you accomplished today only with what you did in the past. If there is any improvement, you are a success. If there is not, you can challenge yourself to do better. Try to ignore what others have done.

■ Keep your faults to yourself...

You may resist all opportunities to feel good about yourself and tell everyone how unworthy you are.Usually, a person repeats self-destructive behavior because he derives benefits from it.

You may minimize your achievements and flaunt your faults to protect other people from being hurt because you believe they will be threatened if they see you as attractive or clever. You may think it is your role in life is to make everyone happy.

You may do it to protect yourself from criticism, because you think that if you say good things about yourself, other people will be jealous and will attack you. The trouble is that people may believe the negative things you tell them about yourself and not think much of you.

You may hide your successes because you think that if you tell people that you are capable, they will pressure you to keep it up or do better. When you act like a failure, people may expect nothing from you, but they will never be proud of you either.

You may put yourself down and say "poor me" so people will feel sorry for you and give you attention. You may think that if you show people that you have confidence, they will ignore you or take you for granted. The problem is that pity is not love, so when you get attention because people feel sorry for you, it doesn't mean they really care about you.

People tend to believe what you say about yourself. If you point your faults out to them and tell them you are stupid or clumsy or crazy, they may think you are. When you say negative things about yourself, people fail to see your good points. If you give people a chance to accept you as you are, you may be surprised to see that they are not as concerned about your flaws as you are.

■ **Accept praise from others...**

If people compliment you, do you try to play it down? If they admire something you are wearing, do you tell them it is old or it was cheap? When you do that, it is the same as saying their judgment is wrong. They like it, but you are telling them that they don't know what they are talking about. If you do that every time they say something flattering, they may get annoyed with you. Try to say "thank you" when you receive praise, whether or not you agree with it.

■ **Treat yourself well...**

When you are good to yourself, you automatically improve your self-image. See if you can treat yourself the way you want others to treat you, and the way you treat those you love. Do it because you deserve it, not because you earned it for some accomplishment. Eat healthy foods, not junk. Give yourself permission to take a rest or a vacation when you need to. Make sure you do things you enjoy, some time every day, if possible. Surround yourself with loving people, and get out of abusive relationships. Avoid doing anything that is self-destructive.

12. ASSERTING YOURSELF

You want your boss, your neighbors, friends, relatives, and your immediate family to treat you with respect, and not be controlling, attacking, blaming, arrogant, unreasonable, demanding, invasive, manipulative, smothering, or violent. If someone does treat you that way, you can say nothing, still feel angry, and then brood about it; you can blame yourself and think you deserve to be mistreated; or you can go after the person mistreating you and be revengeful, manipulative, or abusive.

There is a better way: telling him to stop in an assertive way. According to the dictionary, that means being *persistently positive*. You demand to be treated better, and you do it because you know you have that right. You do it without attacking anyone, and you keep insisting until you get your way.

Rating Your Assertiveness

How assertive are you? Fill out the following chart to find out:

Check the statements that are true for you:	
☐ I feel entitled to be treated well.	☐ I do not feel equal to others.
☐ I confront others when I am angry.	☐ I avoid confronting people.
☐ I say no when I want to.	☐ I have a hard time saying no.
☐ I do only what I want to do.	☐ I do whatever I am asked to do.
☐ I make eye contact when I speak.	☐ I never look people in the eye.
☐ I express my anger without apologizing.	☐ I apologize for my anger.
☐ I communicate my needs to others.	☐ I never say what I want.
☐ I take responsibility for my feelings.	☐ I hide my vulnerability.
☐ I set boundaries on how to be treated.	☐ I let people push me around.

If you checked more of the statements in the right hand list than the one on the left, you need to become more assertive.

Advantages of Being Assertive

What you accomplish by choosing to express your anger in an assertive way is:

■ **No one feels hurt....**

When you are angry and call people names, you attack their self-esteem and they feel hurt. When you blame yourself for mistreatment by others and call yourself names, you hurt yourself. When you are assertive, you express your anger as a firm statement without hurting either yourself or anyone else.

■ **You are listened to...**

When you apologize for your anger or express it timidly, you are not likely to be taken seriously. People ignore you or easily forget what you say. When you yell at others or criticize them, you attack their self-esteem. If they feel threatened, they become defensive, focus on feeling sorry for themselves, and tune out what you say.

When you make an assertive statement, people have no need to protect themselves from being hurt, so they can really listen to what you say.

■ **You are understood....**

When you apologize for being angry, you are not saying what you really mean. When you are hostile, you are attacking instead of talking about your feelings. In both cases, you can easily be misunderstood.

When you are assertive, you tell others exactly what you feel and what you want. Your communication is clear and direct, so there is no chance that what you are saying can be misinterpreted.

■ **You are respected....**

When you come across as passive, people think they can take advantage of you. They usually do not respect you. When that happens, you may lose respect for yourself. When you express your anger in an aggressive way, you may lose control and say something you later regret. People may think you look foolish and not respect you.

When you say something assertively, you do it in a dignified way without losing your temper. You gain respect from others and from yourself.

- **You get what you want..**

When you speak meekly, your requests can easily be ignored. People don't realize that you are serious, or that you will do anything about it if they pay no attention to what you tell them. They know they can get away with it, so they continue to behave as they have.

When you give orders to people in a hostile way, they are not likely to want to comply. In fact, they may want to be vindictive and punish you by doing the opposite of what you want.

When you speak assertively, you sound like you mean what you say. You let others know that you will continue to fight for what you want. They have no need to be defensive because they are not being attacked, so they are more likely to do what you want.

- **Your anger ends...**

When you hide your anger and say nothing, you constantly walk around with it. When you express it too passively, you get ignored and you stay angry.

When you are explosive, your anger escalates. If you make others angry by attacking them, you prolong the battle and both you and they continue to feel angry.

When you are assertive, no one is left feeling hurt or wanting to hurt you. Since you get what you want, you have no more reason to be angry.

Getting Ready

Before you can be assertive with people who mistreat you, you need to believe the following:

- **I can have an impact on other people...**

When you think you have no power, you make requests in a half-baked way and people react accordingly. To approach others in an assertive manner, you have to believe that you can make people listen. You have to have a sense of your own power. After all, you are no less powerful than anyone else. That doesn't mean you have to be big in stature or talk loudly. In fact, that could intimidate others and make them angry. You can quietly make demands and be effective.

■ **I am willing to face rejection...**

Being assertive may not seem to you to be as safe as being passive or aggressive because it involves rocking the boat and maybe being rejected for it. However, it is worth it to have your demands met.

You just have to keep in mind that you really don't have to have everyone's approval. You are likely to get their respect if you are assertive.

■ **I am willing to show that I am vulnerable...**

If you want to look tough, you can put on a facade and not be open. To be assertive, you must be unafraid to reveal your hurt feelings and your imperfections. That does not mean you look weak. In fact, most people are likely to appreciate your sharing your feelings. If they don't, then they are not really people you should have in your life.

Showing your vulnerability is well worth the risk. It results in respect for yourself and in seeing positive change.

■ **I am equal to other people...**

If you feel inferior to other people, you cannot effectively tell them how you feel. Your voice may sound weak, and your protests may come across as tentative. You may find that no one listens to you.

If you feel superior to others, you express your anger in an arrogant manner. People may feel attacked and become defensive. They may want to ignore you or they may want to hurt you. In either case, they are not likely to treat you well.

To be assertive, you first have to feel entitled to be treated well. You have to know that no matter what your age, intelligence, wealth, title, background, skills, gender, or race, you are equal to others in importance and worth. Then, you are able to set limits, establish boundaries, and let people know that they must respect you.

Your Rights as a Person

Before you can stand up for your rights, you have to know what those rights are as a person, a man or woman, a parent, and a consumer. You have certain rights as a citizen of America which are stated in the Bill of Rights, such as liberty and the pursuit of happiness. You also have many rights as a person that may be more much specific than those listed in the Bill of Rights.

Think about what you are entitled to as a human being in all of your roles in life.

List all the rights you think you have:

As a person, I have the right to:

1. _____ 6. _____

2. _____ 7. _____

3. _____ 8. _____

4. _____ 9. _____

5. _____ 10. _____

As a human being, you are entitled to be treated the way you treat others and want to be treated. How many things were you able to list? Was it difficult to think of things because you are not used to feeling entitled to anything? Do you believe you deserve the things on your list?

How many of the following did you mention:

- **The right to privacy.** You have the right to tell people who ask probing questions that you would rather not answer. You don't have to allow anyone to open your mail or touch your possessions without your permission. You can expect people to knock on your door before entering, to make appointments to see you and not just show up unannounced.

- **The right to be treated with respect.** You have a right to talk without being interrupted or attacked for your ideas, and to be spoken to as a worthwhile person. That means you don't get insulted, manipulated or put in any humiliating situation by others.

- **The right to make choices.** You can make decisions about what to eat, what to wear, where to go, how to spend your money, and what to do with your life. You can refuse to do what you don't want to do, as long as no one is harmed. You have a right to object to the behavior of others, and to protest mistreatment.

- **The right to express your feelings.** You are entitled to feel depressed or angry and to say that you do, whether or not others are comfortable with it. To express your anger assertively, it is especially important not to feel guilty about having angry feelings.

- **The right to set emotional boundaries.** You can decide how close you will let people be to you and which people you will have in your life. You have a right to put some distance between you and their problems.

- **The right to make mistakes.** You should not be berated when you make a mistake, nor should you have to defend yourself or apologize for it, as long as no one has been hurt by whatever mistake you have made.

- **The right to time out.** You are entitled to be alone part of every day, as long as you are not neglecting or endangering anyone.

If you could not list very many rights, you probably don't demand very much or get treated very well. Give the list more thought and try to add to it as you go through the week.

Your Rights as a Man or Woman

Gone are the days when society defined exactly what a man or woman could do or say. Now a man may raise a child alone after a divorce; may stay home with a child while his wife works; may be in a love relationship with another man; may raise a child with him. He may cry and show his feelings. A woman may work in most every occupation, dress in unisex clothes or in slinky outfits.

Are there areas in your life in which you feel that you are being treated unfairly because you are a man or a woman? Do you feel that you have any rights as a man or a woman?

List what you think are your rights:

As a man (or a woman), I have the right to:

1. _____

2. _____

3. _____

4. _____

5. _____

What did you say? Did you mention the right to be hired for any job in which you qualify, regardless of your gender? How about the right to react or think differently than someone of the opposite sex? If you are a man, do you think you have as much right as any woman to complain about sexual abuse or misconduct? If you are a woman, can you decide to stay single? If you get pregnant, do you have the right to have an abortion or to decide not to have one? No matter what your gender, you have the right to throw away all of the old stereotypes and be treated as an individual in all areas of your life.

Your Rights as a Parent

Are you a parent? Do you have rights or do you think you are supposed to be a servant to your children? Are you able to set any limits on what they can do, or do you let them call the shots?

List what you think are your rights:

As a parent, I have the right to:

1. _____

2. _____

3. _____

4. _____

5. _____

What did you say? Do you think you should be treated with respect by your children? Do they know that you need privacy, time alone, or time out for yourself? Do you have the right to protect your possessions and expect them to be handled carefully? Do you have the right to expect your children to eventually move out and support themselves?

How you are treated by your children depends on what you demand of them. When you refuse to do certain chores and give your children the responsibility of doing them, you stop being seen as a servant. When you hire sitters and go out or go to work, or work on some project at home, they understand that you are a separate person with a separate life. When you set limits on their behavior, you get their respect. If you don't, you let them abuse you or manipulate you.

Of course, to treat you with respect, your children first have to get respect from you. If you are critical, verbally abusive, or controlling, they will be angry and may be rude and rebellious.

Your Rights as a Consumer

What do you think you are entitled to when you purchase goods and services from stores, restaurants, medical offices, banks, gas stations? What do you expect from clerks, cashiers, waiters, doctors, mechanics, repairmen, or anyone else you hire?

List what you think are your rights:

As a consumer, I have the right to:

1. _____
2. _____
3. _____
4. _____
5. _____

Did you list any of the following?

- **The right to get the product you pay for**. You should not shop in any store that attempts to give you a cheap replacement for a product that was advertised. You should not be sold something that is defective and breaks down soon after you buy it.

- **The right to receive compensation when there is an error.** If you buy a product that does not perform as advertised, you have the right to expect the store or the mail order house to give you a refund or replace the item. If you place an ad in a newspaper and it is printed incorrectly, you have the right to expect the newspaper to run it again without charge.

- **The right to get the service you are paying for.** If you hire a mechanic to fix your car, a plumber to fix your faucet, a painter to paint your house, a waiter to serve you food, or a dentist to fix your teeth, you have the right to expect them to do a good job. If their service is not satisfactory, you have the right to complain or to take your business elsewhere.

• **The right to get accurate information about cost.** If you bring a bunch of bananas to the checkout register in the market, you have a right to be charged the same price per pound that was posted on the sign in the fruit section. If you have dental work, you have a right to expect it to cost the amount you were quoted before the dentist started. You have the right to have the car salesman, the vet, and the doctor tell you in advance what the cost is for their product or services, and what the fee includes. They cannot add on unexpected charges at the last minute or after you have paid the agreed amount.

Before You Make an Assertive Statement

Before you are ready to make a demand of someone, you need to first do the following:

■ **Identify the source of your anger...**

You can only be assertive when you know exactly what it is about someone's behavior that is triggering your anger.

Jerry, 52, felt angry every time his sister came to visit him. He wanted to tell her, but he was not clear what he was angry about. He didn't know if it was because her tone of voice sounded arrogant, because her words seemed critical of him, or because she didn't compliment him.

In counseling, Jerry discovered that although these things did contribute to his anger, they were not the main reason for it. His anger was more about his sister's asking him personal questions that he was not comfortable answering.

■ **Know why it makes you angry...**

When Jerry's sister asked him questions because she was truly interested in things about his life, Jerry remembered how she had barged into his room when they were children. Both situations seemed like an invasion of his privacy. It was not that being asked a question was rude, only that Jerry had a problem with it. His anger had more to do with himself than with his sister.

Being angry is your responsibility, not the other person's. He doesn't make you angry, you choose to react with anger.

Jerry's sister was being friendly, not nosy, when she asked him a question. She didn't know that he was sensitive in this area, so it was not her fault that he got angry. Jerry was responsible for his reactions. He could have been flattered that she cared enough about him to inquire about personal things, instead of resenting it. He was confusing her present questioning with her past behavior.

If Jerry wanted his sister to leave him alone and not question him, he had to tell her. Instead of being somewhat irritable when they met, he had to say, "When you ask me a personal question, it reminds me of how you took my things when we were children. I would rather not share anything about myself now."

To make such a statement, Jerry had to be willing to take responsibility for his anger. Obviously, if his sister continued to be nosy after he asked her not to be, then he could blame her.

How to Be Assertive

If you believe you have rights, you are ready to convey that belief with words, with your tone of voice, your posture, and the way you walk. They all send a message about your credibility and your worth. People believe what they see, so when you act confident, they think what you say is important. When you act like you are worthless, they ignore what you say. To be effective, it is important that the non-verbal messages you give match the words you speak.

To be assertive, you have to:

■ **Keep your body erect...**
When you speak, you want people to listen. You want them to believe you mean what you say. If you are hunched over and have your head down while you are talking, you may seem frightened or insecure, and people may ignore you. Standing makes an even stronger statement than sitting, especially if you are talking to someone who is already standing. It puts you on his level. If he is sitting and you stand, you can seem to have even more authority.

- **Make eye contact with the other person...**

If you look at the floor when you try to speak assertively, your message can get lost and you can seem scared. If you shift your eyes and look around the room when you talk, you can seem evasive. Doing either one can make it hard for the other person to take you seriously.

When you look someone in the eyes, you let him know that you feel strong about what you are saying and that it is important to you. You also tell him that he is the one you are talking to and that he better watch out. Then, he is more apt to listen to your words.

- **Speak calmly...**

When you feel furious, it is not a good time to try to be assertive. You lose respect from the other person when you get hysterical, whine, yell, or lose control, and he is likely to tune you out. It is better to wait until you calm down and can speak in a more unemotional and objective way.

- **Describe the other person's behavior...**

When you tell someone in an assertive way that you are angry, you begin by discussing his actions. You begin the sentence with *When you...* and you tell him what he is doing that upsets you (criticize me, keep your room messy, etc.). You may tell the dentist, the store manager, or the painter about his service or his product; you may tell the waiter about his bringing you food that is cold or too salty.

- **Explain your feelings about what happened...**

You continue the sentence with *then I.....* You say you feel angry, hurt, unloved, rejected, mistreated, taken advantage of. You may be wrong if you think the other person is purposely doing this, but you are not wrong about your feelings.

Assertive statements are I statements, so they are more about you than the other person. They tell about your level of tolerance about a situation, and they don't attack or insult anyone. The other person has no need to become defensive or tune you out.

- **Say what you want...**

Whether you are communicating on a personal level or about business, you have to let the other person know what it is you want and expect. You have to say *I want you to* treat me better or clean your *room* or *give me a refund.*

■ **Sound as if you mean it...**

To be believed, you have to make a statement or a demand. You can't sound apologetic because that will discount whatever you say. If your request sounds like a question, it is as though you are asking for permission to have it. You have to speak in a manner that leaves no room for discussion, for negotiation, or for disagreement.

■ **State your intentions...**

Tell the other person what you plan to do if you don't get what you want: that you will leave; you will see that the other person leaves; you will fire him; you will take him to court; you will complain to the Better Business Bureau or the Consumer Protection Agency; you will report him to his superiors; you will do business elsewhere.... Be sure you mean what you say, that you plan to follow through and are not just making an idle threat.

■ **Repeat and insist...**

People are likely to ignore you the first time you tell them to make some change in their behavior. You may have to say it more than once until they are convinced that you are serious. They would rather continue their behavior and will try to make you back down.

If you are not used to being assertive, it may be hard for you to be insistent. You will find, however, that it does get easier over time. When you stand your ground, people see that you mean what you say. After a while, they fight you less when you want something.

You must be consistent, though. You can't be assertive and demanding about something one day and then submissive about it the next. That gives people the idea that you can easily be talked out of whatever you want.

■ **Take action...**

When you deal with a business establishment rather than with someone you know, you may have to write letters or contact someone in a higher position. If you order something from a store, such as a piece of furniture, and it is defective, tell the manager rather than a salesperson. If you have some problem with a hotel or a hospital, take your complaints to the president, rather than a clerk. If you get poor service in a restaurant, contact the manager, rather than a waiter.

If necessary, go to whatever professional organization deals with the establishment, such as the Bar Association or the American Medical Association. Follow up on threats: go to small claims court, hire an attorney, sue. You have to decide how important it is to you to win, and whether you can afford the time and expense of taking legal action.

It may be simpler to just overlook things that happen. But when you know that you are unfairly being manipulated by some business or service person, it is well worth the effort to take some sort of action. You may win, and even if you don't, you have the satisfaction of having let him know you put up a fight.

To sum up how to make an assertive statement:
- *describe the behavior:* When you _____
- *state your feelings:* then I _____
- *state your needs:* I want you to _____
- *state your intentions:* If you don't, I will _____

Examples

Being assertive is so much more effective than being passive, passive-aggressive, or aggressive, as the following stories indicate:

A woman was unhappy about her husband spending too much time in front of his computer. She felt shut out and lonely, and also angry. She told her husband it was not fair, but he continued to do it.

Because the woman spoke to her husband with a whining complaint, all he heard was that he did something wrong and was being scolded. She would have accomplished much more if she spoke to him assertively and said: "When you spend so much time at the computer, I feel shut out. It seems like you are choosing not to be with me. I don't like having this kind of marriage, and I won't stay around if it continues. I expect you to spend more time with me from now on."

This is a clear statement which would have told him how she felt without his feeling attacked. He would have no reason to be defensive. If he really cared about his wife, he would be sympathetic and make some changes.

In another situation, a woman was angry with her teenage son for frequently leaving his dirty dishes on the table after he ate. Sometimes she said nothing. Other times, she yelled and screamed at him to put them in the sink. He then ran in his room and slammed the door without removing the dirty dishes.

The woman had not found a way to get her son to do what she wanted. She either kept her feelings to herself or she insulted him and made him resentful. She needed to tell him assertively: "When I have to put your dishes in the sink after you eat and rinse them, it gives me extra work. It feels like I'm being taken for granted, and that makes me angry. From now on, I expect you to take care of your dishes yourself." Nothing in this statement is an attack, so her son was likely to be more willing to cooperate.

A middle-aged couple named Ned and Rose were waiting on line to see a popular movie. Ned became angry when a man got in line in front of them. Ned was unwilling to let the man get away with it, so he yelled at him, then threatened him. The man then called him insulting names and refused to move. When the crowd sided with Ned, the man finally went to the end of the line. However, Ned was embarrassed about having created a scene.

Rose, too, was angry with the man, but said nothing. It already upset her that people were looking at them and she didn't want to call more attention to herself. She was also angry with Ned for carrying on, but she was afraid he would get angry with her if she told him that. Then she was angry with herself for keeping quiet.

Ned was being aggressive by screaming at the man. Rose was being passive by ignoring an obvious injustice. If they had been assertive, they would have spoken strongly to the man in a way that was not hostile or threatening, and they would have told him it was unfair to cut in. Ned would not have lost his temper; and he would have received support from Rose, instead of silent disapproval. Maybe the man would not have felt attacked and he would have immediately moved to the back of the line.

Todd, 15, was doing a report for school. He borrowed an expensive book on a related topic from his father and he took a long time returning it. When he finally did, it was soiled, so his father got angry. He became attacking and called him irresponsible and worthless because he assumed his son didn't care about him.

If he had more faith in his son's judgment, he would have asked him what happened in an assertive way without accusing him. Then he would have learned that his son's friend had borrowed the book, accidentally spilled juice on it, and took his time returning it to Todd.

Todd planned to tell his father what happened, but then was intimidated when his father became furious. He anticipated more criticism, so he said nothing. He concluded that his father cared more about the book than about him. Todd gave up the chance to stand up for himself, and that made him feel disappointed in himself.

If Todd had been assertive and told his father that it was not entirely his fault, he would have retained his self-esteem. His father would have known that Todd was not uncaring, and might have apologized for rushing to make assumptions. Todd would have known that his father cared about him. The lines of communication would have stayed open for the future.

Saying No

When you agree to do things you don't want to do, you end up feeling angry. That is why it is crucial to be able to say no when you want to. Being assertive means saying no to someone in a way that tells him you mean it, so he doesn't ask you any more. It does not mean you think no but then say yes. In the long run, it is easier to say what you mean. You feel better, more in control, and you don't have to pretend you like doing something when you don't. When you are able to say no, you get more respect from people.

Can you say no when you want to? Read the description of each of the following situations, then fill in what you would say if they happened to you:

You have a limited amount of excess cash. You are in the middle of dinner and the phone rings. It is someone from a charity calling to ask you for a pledge. You don't feel strongly in favor of the charity.

I say _____

You could say: "This is not a good time for me. Just mail me something." Or you could say "I am not interested" and hang up. After all, they are invading your home and your time by calling.

Later, the phone rings again. It is someone from a carpet cleaning company. He offers you a discount if you agree to let him clean your carpet. You know your carpets are not that dirty, and you don't want to be bothered.

I say _____

You know that you do not want the salesman to come at this time. If you are not forceful, he will keep you on the phone or call again. You save your time and you also save his time when you stop him before he goes into his speech. All you have to say is "I am not interested", and then hang up. He can now call someone else who may decide to use his services. He won't feel hurt because he knows rejection comes with his job.

A charity calls and asks you to collect money from your neighbors. You are very busy, and you don't like to ask your neighbors for money.

I say _____

You could say "You will have to ask someone else. I am not comfortable collecting money from others." Solicitors expect a large percentage of the people they call to turn them down. They cannot survive the job if they take it personally. Besides, you can be sure they will find someone who is willing to do it.

> *You neighbor calls and asks you to take in her mail and water her plants for a week while she is away on vacation. You are not feeling well and consider it an imposition.*
>
> I say _____

Saying no does not make you a bad person. It is also not your problem if your neighbor can't find someone else to do it. You could say "You will have to ask someone else. I would be glad to do it if I could, but right now, I am too sick (or too busy)."

> *A relative calls and says she will be in town on the weekend and wants to stay overnight in your home. You are not that thrilled with her, and you do have other plans. You also prefer your privacy.*
>
> I say _____

You could say "I already have plans. I will call you when I am free." You need not feel bad because she should not be inviting herself in the first place. If you really don't want her to ever come but you don't want to say so that clearly, you can wait until she calls next time. Then, you can make up some excuse. If you do that every time she calls, she may get tired of asking you.

> *Someone you love makes constant demands. You are tired, and you were hoping to have some time to yourself.*
>
> I say _____

You could say, " I wish I could do everything you want, but I can't. Right now, I am too busy. That doesn't mean I don't love you. I will do it later, but I'm getting tired from doing so much." This helps your family put their needs in prospective, and helps them learn that they are not the only ones with needs. It also keeps you from feeling resentful toward them.

> *You let your adult daughter move back into your house when she loses her job. She sleeps late, is disorganized, takes drugs, and keeps asking for money. You don't want this.*
>
> I say_____

You could say, "I am not happy with this arrangement. I feel trapped, taken for granted, unappreciated, and manipulated. Unless you make some drastic changes and take charge of your life, you will have to leave."

When someone is dependent on you in any way, you may like being needed and important to him. However, you have a right to decide under what conditions you will be generous, and it is not unreasonable to expect him to pull his share of the load.

You should not take on a caretaking position unless you are able to set limits in terms of your money, time, and freedom. Otherwise, you end up resenting or even hating your crying baby, sick child, frail mother, ailing spouse. You need to do the following:

- Set limits on the amount of time and money you will give. If you are asked for more, say no and don't back down.

- Voice your need for appreciation and positive feedback. If you aren't getting any, threaten to quit.

- Take time out for yourself, no matter how busy you are. Do something you enjoy at some time each day.

- Set limits on which tasks you will perform and which you won't. No need to feel guilty if you can't do it all.

- Hire a professional nurse or sitter if at all possible, so you don't feel burdened.

If you do these things, you are less likely to be angry at the person who is dependent on you.

There is nothing wrong with saying no. It is not necessary to make a pledge, buy products, or do errands for others when you don't want to. You are entitled to have a life, to have needs, and to make decisions about your time and your energy.

It is not rude to say no. You can be honest and people will accept it if you say it in a way that is final, without apologizing or leaving room to be persuaded. You don't owe anything to anyone, so there is no reason to feel guilty about it.

You also don't have to worry about what people will think of you if you say no. Those who call to ask for money don't even know you and will never see you. Those who do know you have no right to push you after you say no. They need to respect your wishes and understand you are not mean if you don't want to do something.

It is hardly ever true that if you don't help out, there will be no one else to help. What happens, though, if you always say yes to people you know, they come to expect it and may take advantage of you.

The best thing to do is to begin saying no with people you trust and see what happens. If it works, try it with other people. You will find that it is much easier than you thought it would be and that it makes your life so much easier.

Assertiveness as Reinforcement

If you want someone's behavior to change, it is important to tell him when he is doing something right, not only when he is doing something wrong. Always yelling and scolding about what you don't like does not give the other person a clue about what you want. You may think it is obvious to him, but it may not be.

You want the positive behavior to continue, so you have to give feedback when it occurs. Your sentences can begin with the phrase "I like it when you..." or "Thank you for..." and end with "I hope you will do it again." If you are angry that someone living with you has his personal belongings all over the house, you need to praise him if he suddenly cleans up. If he is usually abusive and suddenly becomes affectionate, you need to tell him you noticed the difference. When someone is praised for his actions, he is more motivated to repeat them than if he only gets scolded for doing something wrong.

13. TAKING CHARGE

Breaking Out of Traps

Feeling trapped threatens your freedom and control, you think the situation will never end, and you feel helpless, frustrated, and angry. If you could avoid being in all situations in which you feel trapped, you would have one less thing triggering your anger.

There are some trapped situations over which you have no control: having to take care of a child with an illness, deformity, or handicap; being laid up with a disease; being stuck in traffic; being shut in due to a snowstorm. They happen without anyone causing them, and are not the result of a plot by anyone to hurt you. There is no one to blame, so anger is not appropriate and accomplishes nothing. All you can do is accept the fact that you cannot do anything about them.

Most of the time, you end up in a trapped situation of your own doing. You can't blame anyone else for putting you there. Instead of brooding about it, you have to see the situation for what it is and consider all aspects of it.

Do you feel trapped in any area of your life, such as your job or a relationship you are in? At whom is your anger directed? Do you blame your boss, your partner, your children, your parents, society, or anyone else? You can help yourself by asking yourself the following questions:

■ **Is this situation temporary or permanent?**

Molly and her husband were in their sixties and had been enjoying life without their children in the house. Then, their son finished college and could not find a job, and their daughter got divorced, had to work, and needed someone to stay with her baby. They both asked their parents if they could stay in their house temporarily.

Molly agreed to let them both move back in, but she was furious all the time because she thought it would go on forever. She felt trapped, so she was grouchy and disagreeable, and she picked on them.

Molly focused on seeing every decision as a forever thing, instead of as the most practical solution for the moment. It would have been more productive for Molly to put her energy into ways to help her son and daughter get on their feet and get out.

Many situations are temporary and will come to an end or improve with time, and knowing that can help you be less angry. Your boss may be replaced, your dependent children will grow up, and your baby will stop screaming.

■ What are my alternatives?

Linda was married to an abusive man. He either criticized her or completely shut her out. He never considered her feelings and never spent time with her. Linda wanted to leave and get a divorce, but she had no money and did not expect to get any from her husband. She stayed because she had many fears about leaving, and she failed to see that she had many alternatives:

- To stay married and insist on a joint bank account so she could be more independent. Since she had never asked her husband for it, she didn't really know how he would react.

- To get a separation before considering a divorce, so she could experience being alone. It is always better to take a small step than a big one.

- To stay married and insist her husband come to counseling with her and work on the conflicts.

- To get a good attorney to help her file for a divorce with an equal settlement.

- To go to work to have some income of her own, then find a small apartment to experience living alone.

- To move in temporarily with a friend to gain some perspective on the situation and distance herself from the abuse.

- To stay married but date other men to gain a basis of comparison and feel stronger.

It is rare to find a situation that has no way out. If you feel trapped, sit down and make a list of all the things you can do. If you hate your job, you could leave and try to get another job, you could stay and confront your boss, or you could take the problem to Human Resources. If you can't stand being in the house so much with your children, you could hire a sitter and get out, you could call a friend with children and take turns sitting, or you could go somewhere with your children. If you feel trapped in a destructive relationship, you could try to end it, or stay in it and go to counseling.

■ **Am I afraid to make a change?**

Linda was trapped by her fears, assumptions, and lack of information, not by her situation. She was afraid of being alone, of meeting new men, and of working. She thought she would end up with a man worse than her husband. So she would stay with her husband until the situation was unbearable to her or until she felt strong enough to leave.

What thoughts keep you from leaving your job, your marriage, or your relationship with someone? Is the idea of leaving too scary? Do you think you will never find another job or have another relationship if you leave? Are you staying to protect your boss or your mate from experiencing any pain? Your fears and beliefs may be based on distortions and not on reality, and staying in the situation may not be better than dealing with the consequences of leaving.

Are you a caretaker to an elderly, sick, helpless, or emotionally fragile family member? Do you want to do it? Does it make you angry? Is there anyone else who could do it? Are there any alternatives? Are you doing this because you like being indispensable? What will you do if this person mistreats you while you are taking care of him? You might want to seek legal, financial, or psychological counseling to clarify the facts about the situation.

■ **Am I staying in by choice?**

Carol lived in a large house in the suburbs with her husband and her son. The house was expensive to maintain, and her husband used whatever he earned for household expenses. If they moved to a smaller house, they would have extra money, but he refused.

Carol wanted their son, who was a high school junior, to go to a good college next year, so she was working to pay for it. She hated her job and wanted to pursue another career, but her money was needed, so she kept working.

Carol felt trapped and blamed her husband for putting her in this position. She complained that everyone in the family was going to get what they wanted except her.

Carol did not see that this situation was **temporary**, limited to the time that her son would be in college or until her husband's business prospered.

She also forgot that she had **alternatives**:

- She could send her son to a less expensive school and have money left to pursue her career. That required giving up the notion that a cheaper school wouldn't provide him with a good education, and that she was a terrible parent if she provided less than the best for him. The fact was that Carol's son did not care what college he attended, and neither did her husband.

- She could send her son to school part-time and have him work to supplement the costs. She might have to work part-time too, but she could also take courses. Both Carol and her son had to make compromises.

- She could wait to send her son to college, and have him work until he could pay for it. Then, she could quit her job and pursue the career she wanted. This meant placing her needs first, something Carol had never done.

- She could insist that they move to a less expensive house so there would be extra money and she would not need to work. That meant being very assertive with her husband, which Carol was not used to doing.

Carol had put herself in the situation and had made the choice to stay in it. By not making her needs as important as where her son would go to school, she avoided feeling guilty. By not demanding they move, she avoided her husband's anger. When Carol realized all this, she stopped blaming anyone and was less angry.

Being Dependent

When you are completely dependent on someone else for financial support, emotional support, pleasure and excitement, health care, or basic needs, you may experience a loss of freedom and control. Then, you may get angry about needing to be taken care of.

Herb, 56, had severe back pain as the result of a fall and depended on his wife for everything. He could no longer work, drive, or walk for very long. He was angry with everyone because he was so helpless, and took much of that anger out on his wife. He ordered her around, making many demands when he could not get something himself. Then, he criticized her for not doing things exactly as he wanted them done.

Herb's wife knew she had to do things for him, and would not have resented it if he had not been so angry and critical all of the time.

It is hard enough to feel good about yourself when you cannot get what you need without someone else's help because you are ill, handicapped, emotionally frail. You make the situation worse when you blame your caretaker.

When you depend on someone for something, you may think that he knows what you need, that he wants to give it to you, and that he will always be there. Since he is only human, he is bound to let you down. He cannot read your mind about what you want, so he may get it wrong. He has needs of his own, so he may resent taking care of you at times. The more unrealistic your expectations, the more disappointed and angry you may be.

When you rely on him for money, love, pleasure, or nurturing, you endow him with power. Instead of getting it yourself, you have to wait for him to give it to you. If he is incompetent, lazy, mean, tired, or angry, he can decide to take it away. The more you put your happiness or your survival in his hands, the more you feel helpless and beholden to him, and the angrier you may get.

You may also get angry with the other person for putting you in a bind.

Freddie was 16 and depended on his parents to pay for gas, new clothes, or going out with a friend. He knew there were strings attached to their helping him. If he was disagreeable, rebellious, or insulting to them, they refused to give him any money or let him use the car. He tried not to antagonize them, but he felt compromised, and this made him angry.

Fortunately for Freddie, his parents did not take advantage of him.

They encouraged him to verbalize his feelings without attacking, and they did not punish him for it. At the same time, they could not be blamed for cutting off all help if he did become abusive to them.

Declaring Your Independence

If you are completely dependent on others for everything you need, including money, fun, and love, you can be very angry when they don't come through for you. To be less angry, you need to set your life up so that you are hardly dependent on anyone. That means doing the following:

- **Make your own decisions...**

Are you a leader or a follower? When you go with friends to a movie or a restaurant and they ask you where you want to go, do you know, or do you wait to see what they say? When you have to make a major decision, do you wait to see what other people think? Do you take their advice, or do you come to your own conclusions? Do you do what they say and then blame them if it doesn't turn out well?

If you make your own decisions, they are more likely to be the right ones for you. You know better than anyone else what is best for you, and your intuition will tell you what to do. When you can't decide on something, consider all the options, consider the probable outcomes of each, but then do what feels right.

- **Initiate relationships...**

If you feel lonely, it is up to you to do something about it. You cannot expect to give all that responsibility to others.

Lila, 55, was divorced and had lived alone for the past twenty years. Although she had a car, a condominium, and a job, she saw herself as helpless. She had few friends, no dates, and never called anyone to go anywhere with her. She waited until they called her, and if they didn't, she sat home and brooded. She was bitter toward the world for ignoring her.

Lila did nothing to make her situation better. She was still angry with her parents for having neglected her when she was a child, and she was trying to get others to make it up to her. She craved love and attention, but did nothing to put people in her life.

She needed to reach out to others, make phone calls, have a party, answer ads to meet men, go to workshops, take a trip with a group. Instead, she depended on others for her happiness. Only when she put her anger aside could she take charge of her life.

Do you have enough people in your life? Do you do anything to change it? Do you reach out to people, or do you wait for them to come to you? Do you go to parties and start a conversation? Do you make phone calls and extend invitations to others, or do you wait for people to call you?

When people don't call you, it is not always because of disinterest. There could be other reasons, so you need to see what happens if you make the next call. When you call the shots, instead of others, you feel a lot less angry.

■ **Become financially independent...**

Ted, 32, was single, with no one to support but himself. He had a well-paying job, a modest apartment and earned enough to pay his expenses. However, he was always in debt and acted almost like a homeless person. He hung around where his friends lived and got served meals. When he agreed to go to the movies or to a restaurant, he often showed up with no money in his pocket and had some excuse about not having gone to the bank. The friend usually paid for him, and Ted always "forgot" to pay him back. Most of his friends didn't realize what Ted was doing. Those who did got mad and dropped him.

Ted used his credit cards to pay for expensive electronic equipment he didn't need or couldn't afford. This compulsive spending put him in debt, which he didn't like, but he did nothing to change it because it gave him other things he needed. He could be dependent on others for financial support and he could get attention from them.

When Ted was unhappy about what he was doing, he went for counseling and learned better ways to get love and attention. He also went to a financial consultant and learned how to manage his money.

Do you earn money? Is it in your own bank account, or in a joint account with someone? Do you give part of it to someone in your family? You can only be independent if you have your own money and can do what you want with it.

You may have to depend on someone to pay for your food, rent, clothing, and other expenses because you are a full-time student, are disabled or ill, have to take care of a young child, or because you are out of a job and unable to find another one.

If you find that your financial dependence on someone is causing conflicts and anger, discuss with that person what can be done to remove some of the tension between you. The more clear cut are the terms for giving money to you, the less anger or misunderstanding there will be. If the situation is temporary, you have to try not to be angry while you wait it out.

- **Take charge of your body...**

If you have a serious illness or injury and cannot get around by yourself, you are forced to depend on someone else for care. If you don't wish to hire a caretaker or cannot afford one, you may become dependent on your family. That can produce a lot of tension for everyone, because they may resent your making demands, and you may resent their not always meeting your demands.

You don't, however, have to be totally dependent on the medical community. You have to take charge of your own body and do the following:

- **Choose your doctor.** Ask friends, relatives, and neighbors for recommendations, then interview any doctor whose name comes up frequently. Ask him questions about his background, his methods. Evaluate his manner and if you are uncomfortable with him, find someone else.

- **Become well-informed about your condition.** Read all you can. See how your doctor wants to treat it, then get a second opinion. Find out about alternative treatments, and decide what to do.

- **Evaluate your medication.** If you have to take any, be very aware of all side effects and report them immediately to your doctor. If his solution is to increase the dosage, to ignore what you tell him, or to give you another medication to counteract that one, change doctors and maybe see what the alternative medical community has to offer.

- **Help yourself heal.** Close your eyes and picture the good organisms in your body fighting and destroying the harmful ones. Then conjure up an image of yourself all well. Do this repeatedly until you recover. Strengthen your body's defenses by eating nutritious food, avoiding caffeine, fat, sugar and additives; rest when you are tired; meditate to be as relaxed as you can. Do things you enjoy, like reading or artwork. Focus on pleasure. Accept the situation instead of fighting it. This puts less stress on your body and gives it more energy for healing.

14. REDUCING STRESS

Feeling stressed can make you more irritable and impatient than usual. Most of your stress probably comes from interacting with people and having to deal with their behavior. Sooner or later, many of them leave you feeling rejected, disappointed, frustrated, confused, manipulated, deceived, smothered, or abused.

Getting rid of the stress in your life can make you less angry. To avoid the stress created by people, you would have to completely stop talking to them and stop caring about them. You cannot make them behave in the way you want at all times. If you want people in your life, all you can do is change your reaction to what they do.

There are two stressful conditions which you can avoid because they are probably being created by you: feeling deprived, and feeling rushed and pressured. Since you make yourself feel deprived or rushed, you can work on making changes so they are no longer causes of stress.

You could feel deprived or pressured because of some circumstances beyond your control, but the concern here is about when there are no extenuating circumstances. Then, your stress cannot be blamed on other people.

Taking Care of Your Needs

A contented person is not an angry person. If you feel deprived, you think something is missing from your life, and you are disagreeable and angry with everyone. Your deprivation could be the fault of fate, but it could be because you don't allow yourself to have what you want. It could be that you want too much.

You can prevent your being deprived by taking care of all of your needs, and by changing some of your ideas.

Do you feel deprived? What do you need more of in your life?

Put a check next to the items that indicate what you need:

material things: ☐ possessions ☐ money

power: ☐ prestige ☐ looks ☐ luck ☐ privacy ☐ freedom

love: ☐ affection ☐ attention ☐ recognition ☐ approval ☐ understanding

pleasure: ☐ fun ☐ free time

Did you check more than one thing? Are you angry about not having it? What did you need when you were a child? Is it similar to what you need now?

Who or what is stopping you from having this? Is it you? Do you do anything to get what you need? Are you successful? You can help yourself by doing the following :

■ **Go after what you need...**

When you were a child, you had little ability to get what you needed. You had to wait for your parents to give you everything. If they didn't have enough money, there was nothing you could do. If you wanted more love and support from them, you had no way to get it. If you wanted to go anywhere, you had to wait for them to take you.

It is different now. You are responsible for satisfying your needs. It is not up to others to do it for you. Instead of getting angry, you have to take an active role. If you need more money, you may have to change your job, go back to school to learn a new skill or qualify for a new career. If you are lonely, you have to reach out to people, go to activities, join organizations.

If you need more **privacy** in your life, there are many things you can do.

- When you eat in a restaurant, you can ask to sit at a table away from smokers, loud talkers, or crying babies. You can try to dine at an hour that is quieter, and avoid any place that is crowded.

- You can tell salesclerks in a store that you don't want any help and prefer to shop by yourself.

- You can tell your friends when you want to be alone.

- You can go alone on trips; drive instead of going by train, plane, or bus; avoid tours; stay at a motel on a quiet road rather than a hotel in a downtown area.

- You can choose to live in a less populated area, where there are not a lot of people.

■ **Get love from several sources...**

James, 70, was retired and wanted his wife with him all the time, at home or when he went out. He felt deprived because she had a busy life. She was doing volunteer work, had joined several organizations, and had new friends.

James had no friends and no hobbies. During their forty years of marriage, his wife had never worked and had been dependent. He was not used to the changes in her, and he became jealous and angry when she went out.

Unless James developed some interests of his own and found some other people besides his wife to give him support, he would continue to be possessive. This could make his wife feel smothered and could destroy the marriage.

You also may be creating stress for yourself by expecting one person to fulfill all of your needs. When you do that, you can feel threatened any time that person focuses on his own needs. No one can give you everything you want, so it is better to have several caring people in your life.

■ **Consider that you deserve to have what you want.**

When Jane was a child and got a grade in school below an A, her father was angry with her. Both her parents often evaluated her clothes, her friends, and her athletic abilities as well. She grew up to believe that her worth was based on her performance.

At 28, Jane equated her worth with her ability to get thin. When she stuck to a diet, she thought she earned the right to buy herself something, like shoes or jewelry. If she binged, she was angry with herself and thought she deserved nothing.

Since she was not able to keep her weight at the level she wanted, Jane often denied herself the things she wanted. That meant she felt deprived most of the time. When she did, she felt sorry for herself. Then, she binged to reward herself, and started the whole cycle again.

Jane binged in response to feeling deprived. If she had allowed herself to buy an item unconditionally, not as a reward for good behavior, then she probably would not have felt deprived. As a result, she would have been able to limit her eating.

What do you have to be or do to think you deserve anything? Do you have to be the best, the richest, the most attractive? Do you have to suffer before you can be rewarded? Try giving yourself something without setting up conditions for it. As long as no one gets hurt in the process, you have a right to have what you want. You don't have to earn that right.

■ **Be satisfied with less...**

Appreciate and focus on what you have rather than on what is missing. See if you get angry and bitter when you see people who have more of something than you. Envy and greed can destroy you.

You can make yourself miserable by wishing you looked like the models in a magazine or the stars in the television soaps. Unless you have a job that requires fabulous looks, it makes no difference if you don't have them. The people who love you don't care, nor would they love you more if you had perfect features.

You really don't need a lot to be happy. In fact, suddenly having everything will not guarantee your being happier than you are now. Some people feel rich with very little, and some people with great wealth feel deprived. You can make yourself miserable by wishing you had a million dollars and could afford everything you see. You miss out on enjoying what you do have when you focus on what you don't have.

■ **Communicate your needs to others...**

No one can read your mind and know what you need, so if you don't ask for something, you are not likely to get it. Even then, there is no guarantee that people will always give you what you want. If you ask your family for more love and support and you don't get it, then you have to look elsewhere. Before you assume that is necessary, however, be sure that you have really voiced your needs to them in a very clear way.

Satisfying Your Need for Pleasure

Another way you can feel deprived is when you don't have enough pleasure in your life. If it makes you angry, it is up to you to structure your life so that pleasure is not missing from it.

Are you enjoying yourself? Are you bored? If you have a job or have responsibilities as a student or a parent, you still have some time every day to pursue pleasurable activities. If you think you don't, it may be that your attitude about pleasure is getting in the way and you have to change it. Do you view pleasure as dessert, so you only allow yourself to experience it after you have completed your chores? Of course, chores never end, so you never get to the fun.

Do you see pleasure as forbidden fruit and sinful? Do you feel guilty any time you indulge yourself? Do you think you are lazy and unproductive if you take time off to do nothing? Do you think every moment of the day has to be spent in a productive way? Do you view pleasure as a waste of time?

The fact is that a life with only work and no pleasure is very dull. It even makes you less productive. Your day needs to be balanced between work and play, because playing gives your body a chance to recover from the work. "Lazy" activities such as napping and meditating help you get in touch with your feelings, your intuition, and your creativity. You actually do your work better when your day includes a balance of work and play:

COMBINE		
WORK		**PLAY**
chores	with	fun, pleasure
structure	with	spontaneity
mental activity	with	physical activity
productivity	with	laziness
rationality	with	emotionality

Everything on this list can be considered a necessity, not a frill, and should be done every day.

Do you know what you enjoy doing? Fill out the following chart to determine how much pleasure you have in your life:

List the things you love to do:

_____   _____

_____   _____

_____   _____

_____

Put a check next to all those you have done recently.

Put an x next to those you have never done.

I haven't done the others because _____

How many things did you name that you love to do? Was it hard to think of more than a few? Did you say you love to read, talk on the phone, do crossword puzzles, do jigsaw puzzles, paint, sew, sculpt, play an instrument, play sports, write, exercise, cook, go to parties, go to the theater or the movies, walk, go to the beach, swim, shop, eat, dance, make love?

How many of them have you done recently? How often do you do any of these activities? Are there some you have never done? If you have many more X's than checks, you must not be having much fun in your life.

If you hardly ever do something pleasurable, or if it has been a long time since you did, what is the reason? Are you in a situation beyond your control that keeps you too busy for pleasurable activities, such as having to take care of an infant? Are you just involved in so many activities that you have no time left for ones that you would rather do? Maybe it's your own fault because you have over-committed yourself. If so, you have to rethink your life and see about making some changes.

Slowing Down

Another situation that causes stress and can lead to your feeling angry is being in a hurry and feeling pressured. Sometimes, you can't help it. You may work in a place that gives you deadlines, and the day may not be long enough to meet them. You know that the faster you work, the better your chance of finishing. You may get things in the mail that have to be answered by a certain date. You may have people in your life who need you to make a decision about something within a time frame. The more complex the society you live in, the more complex your life and the more pressures you have.

You can be less stressed and feel less angry if you make some changes:

■ **Change your attitude about time...**

How pressured you feel comes primarily from your belief system. It determines your reaction when you experience a delay or when there are any obstacles to moving as fast as you would like. If you view time as something to beat, if you consider moving fast to be a plus and moving slowly as a negative, you become impatient when things don't move fast. That can only make you tense and angry, since many things can get in the way of hurrying: traffic, bad weather, accidents, construction, phone calls.

Look at the statements in the following exercise and see how you feel about time.

Check those statements that are true for you:

☐ I look at my watch all day.

☐ When I buy merchandise in a supermarket or a department store, I spend several minutes figuring which is the shortest line for paying. After I pick one, it always seem that the others are moving faster.

☐ When I have to pay a toll on a highway, I keep switching from one line to another to get to the one that moves the fastest. It always seem that the one I pick has a driver ahead who is asking questions and delaying my turn.

☐ When I drive on a highway, I weave in and out to get ahead. I usually drive in the left lane to be able to go fast.

☐ I always drive faster than the speed limit.

☐ I get angry if I am unable to beat the red light and have to sit and wait for it to change.

☐ I clock any trip I make in a car to see if I beat the time it usually takes to get there.

☐ I feel upset if I think I lost time in the day with unforeseen events.

☐ I get angry if I make a phone call and am put on hold.

Do you see that you are often impatient about waiting for anything? Are you usually frantic about getting somewhere fast? If so, you can help yourself to slow down if you stop looking at the clock.

Do you have a clock in every room, on your wrist, and in the car? Is the time on most of the clocks digital, showing a moment in time? Is it analog, showing the passage of time? An analog clock is more realistic because it tells you that time is a continuum.

When you say you have lost time, what do you mean? Where did it go? What do you think you should have done with it? Whether you look at a digital clock or an analog clock, you see arbitrary measurements for an abstract concept. When you realize that seconds, minutes, days, weeks, months, and years are not real things, you may be able to slow down more easily.

Is it really necessary to have so many timepieces? Do you even need one at all? Why do you need to know what time it is? If you had to, you could accurately guess the time without looking at a clock. Try doing that at various times throughout the day. You will probably find that your estimation is right.

■ **Be a time manager...**

Your habits and your daily routine also affect the amount of pressure you have. You can make a conscious effort to change them, and that will help you to slow down. You then avoid experiencing some of the situations that lead to your anger.

Do you tend to misjudge the amount of time you need to get ready for an appointment and get up late? Do you misjudge the amount of time it takes to get there and leave late? If you do these things, you are causing yourself to feel rushed.

When you are in a hurry to get somewhere, any obstacle you encounter will upset your schedule and make you angry. If your habits lead to having to hurry, you have to change them. The next time you have an appointment, make an effort to get up earlier, so you can be dressed and ready long before you have to leave. Then leave early to get there with plenty of time to spare. Being early will never make you tense or angry, and being on time will make your life much easier. You will feel more relaxed and have less hassle in your day.

■ **Do things that calm you...**

You help yourself when you avoid substances that speed up your adrenaline, like the caffeine in coffee, chocolate, and cola; or any foods with sugar. Dairy foods have calcium, which is calming, and high fiber foods like brown rice and other whole grains are complex carbohydrates, which also help keep you calm.

You can do activities that are calming, like meditation and exercise. You can buy and use relaxation tapes, and be sure that you get plenty of sleep. When you are calm, you are more tolerant and less apt to take things personally.

■ **Make use of waiting time...**

In any situation that is beyond your control, you can feel trapped and angry. Focusing on how unfair life is *really* wastes your time and keeps you angry. Do you count the minutes spent waiting in traffic, at the airport, at the bank or the doctor's office and feel upset when they add up? Do you consider any extra time it takes to do something a waste?

Instead of getting all frazzled, you can make the time you have to wait anywhere be productive. When you are driving and you get stuck in traffic, you can play tapes to hear music or to learn a foreign language. When you get stuck on a long line at the bank or the market, you can observe what people are wearing. When you know ahead of time that you are going to have to wait somewhere, such as at a doctor's office, you can bring a crossword puzzle or a magazine or a book.

■ **Move slower...**

If you are in a hurry, you can miss seeing things when they happen. When you focus on getting somewhere, you don't see the sights along the way. It is true that when you are late you have to hurry. But hurrying can become a habit, and then, even when you are not late and really have loads of time, you may find you are still rushing. In that case, you have to make a strong effort to slow yourself down. What you can do to make sure you slow down is:

• **Drive in the right lane** and instead of watching the speedometer and the traffic, look at the trees, the sky, the houses, the other cars. Make it into a game the way children do: how many red cars, how many

Hondas, etc.

- **Slow down when you are walking** in the country and look at the trees, the birds, the sky; when you are in the city, look at the people, the buildings, and the shops. Even if you are walking to a destination, pay attention to the sights along the way.

- **Make time to think about your life** and to feel your feelings. Otherwise, you get caught up in less important things and you almost cease to exist.

- **Eat more slowly.** If necessary, put the fork down between bites. When you eat fast, there is not enough time for your stomach to send a message to your brain that it is full, so you can end up eating more than you need. When you rush to finish a meal, you cannot taste the food. Try holding each mouthful of food on your tongue for a few seconds and tuning in to the taste.

- **Breathe deeply and slowly** to slow down your system. People who are in a hurry tend to breathe too fast.

Remind yourself that you are not in any race, and you get no prize for being the fastest. On the contrary - you do yourself more physical and psychological harm when you go fast than when you go slow. Take it easy! You will see more and enjoy life more, and you'll be less angry!

Letting Go

When you are tense, you react with anger to everything that happens. You overlook nothing, and you make an issue about everything. When you do that, you create more tension for yourself. In order to stay calm, not take everything personally and be less angry you need to let go of doing all the following:

■ Let go of fixing...

When you see people who are unhappy or are in trouble, you may think you have to make their lives better. You may think that when one of your children is upset, it is up to you take the upset away. If someone has trouble doing something, you may think you have to jump right in and show him how to do it.

People learn from their mistakes, and children become better functioning adults when they have the opportunity to solve their own problems. It is not your job to fix anything for anyone, and you will have less stress when you give it up.

- **Let go of criticism...**

Instead of being intolerant of people's faults and criticizing them for everything they do, let them be who they are. Try to overlook the things they do that don't fit your qualifications. They are not going to change anyway, so you might as well stop aggravating yourself over it. You will be much more relaxed when you are around people.

- **Let go of paranoia...**

Stop assuming people are trying to hurt you. Every time you do, your body tenses up to counterattack, and the people you accuse get angry. If you are wrong about them, the tension you feel is all for nothing.

It is not likely that you are often right about being attacked, because people are not intentionally destructive very often. Most of the time, their actions are about their own issues, and not about their issues with you. Give people the benefit of the doubt when they do things and find out what has motivated their behavior.

- **Let go of narcissism...**

You can drive people away when you are overly focused on yourself, and when you always have to be the center of attention. If you expect everyone to think you are very special, you can be very disappointed and angry when you discover that most of them have not given it a thought.

It is self-centered to think that people always act in ways to hurt you. If it were true, it would mean that you were on their minds at all times. That is just as unrealistic as believing they think you are great. Most people are more focused on themselves than on you.

If you treat yourself well, you won't need as much from others and you won't be so upset if anyone doesn't make a big fuss about you.

- **Let go of blame and denial...**

Take responsibility for your feelings and your actions. Stop holding others responsible for them. Other people cannot be blamed if you feel angry, sad, or hurt, or if you lose your temper. You create the internal